Make-A-Wish Foundation®

Make-A-Wish® grants wishes to children under the age of 18 with life-threatening medical conditions.

All of the original letters collected for *Celebrating Success* have been donated to the Make-A-Wish Foundation®. They will be sold at several auctions with the proceeds going to assist the organization in its efforts. In addition, $ .50 from the sale of this book will be donated to the Make-A-Wish Foundation. If you are interested in bidding on any letter in the collection, please call (800) 722-9474 before October 1997.

For more information on the Make-A-Wish Foundation and qualifying children, please contact a Make-A-Wish chapter office or call (800) 722-9474.

Inspiring Personal Letters on the Meaning of Success

Compiled by
Gerard Smith

Health Communications, Inc.
Deerfield Beach, FL
www.hci-online.com

Library of Congress Cataloging-in-Publication Data

Cataloging-in-Publication data is available from the Library of Congress.

©1997 Gerard Smith
ISBN 1-55874-455-X (trade paper) — ISBN 1-55874-470-3 (hardcover)

Publisher: Health Communications, Inc.
         3201 S.W. 15th Street
         Deerfield Beach, FL 33442-8190

Cover design by Sue Grimsley

Dedicated to my parents,
who taught me that everyone can be successful—
whatever our definition of success may be!

And to my sister and brothers—
Corinne, Otto and Eric—
who proved it!

And to all people everywhere
who have a desire to achieve success in their lives!

Success is not a destination,
but a journey.

CONTENTS

FOREWORD

Who among us does not want success? No matter what our age, background or position in life, we all desire to fulfill our dreams.

The people in this book are names you will recognize. They are actors, artists, athletes, authors, entertainers, entrepreneurs, heads of state, musicians, religious leaders and scientists. They offer to you their personal definition of success—each as unique as the individual who wrote it.

Success, you see, is available to everyone. We each enter this life endowed with unique gifts. I believe that it is our responsibility to discover this uniqueness and share it with the world, just as the participants in this very special project have done. Our gifts, and talents, one recognizes, are our road maps to success.

It needs to be our objective, therefore, to ask ourselves, "How am I unique?" Sometimes others can help us in our quest. Often our colleagues, friends, relatives and loved ones readily see what makes us special and important.

We need to continually ask ourselves questions about who we are and where we are headed, what gives our life meaning and purpose. We need to take the time to invest in ourselves to become strong and grow spiritually, emotionally and intellectually.

I define success as the freedom to live out my destiny as a speaker, writer, promoter, marketer and visionary entrepreneur. Every individual in this book has discovered and harvested his or her uniqueness. Each has set an example for us to follow. These individuals tell us that success is not out of reach—it is available to us all with focus, perseverance and faith. Enjoy reading their responses. Let them be the springboard from which you will leap to grasp your own dream, your own rising star.

Enjoy your uniqueness. Soon you will call it your success.

—**Mark Victor Hansen**
coauthor of the *Chicken Soup for the Soul* series

INTRODUCTION

I have a thought-provoking composition hanging in my office. It reminds me that everyone defines success from his or her own unique perspective. It reads as follows:

Success

Whatever your mind can conceive and believe, it will achieve. Dream great dreams and make them come true. Do it now. You are unique. In all the history of the world there was never anyone else exactly like you, and in all the infinity to come there will never be another you. Never affirm self-limitations. What you believe yourself to be you are. To accomplish great things, you must not only act, but also dream, not only plan, but also believe. If you have built castles in the air, your work need not be lost; put foundations under them. Yes you can. Believing in magic. You can always better your best. You don't know what you can do until you try. Nothing will come of nothing. If you don't go out on a limb, you're never going to get the fruit. There is no failure except in no longer trying. Hazy goals produce hazy results. Clearly define your goals. Write them down, make a plan for achieving them, set a deadline, visualize the results and go after them. Just don't look back unless you want to go that way. Defeat may test you; it need not stop you. If at first you don't succeed, try another way. For every obstacle there is a solution. Nothing in the world can take the place of persistence. The greatest mistake is giving up. Wishing will not bring success, but planning, persistence, and a burning desire will. There is a gold mine within you from which you can extract all the necessary ingredients. Success is an attitude. Get your right. It is astonishing how short a time it takes for very wonderful things to happen. Now, show us the colors of your rainbow.

—Barbara Smallwood and Steve Kilborn
©1981 Art 101 Limited

Our contributors graciously took the time to share their thoughts on what success means to them based on their own lives. My hope is that you will enjoy reading each definition and take the time to reflect on its meaning, both from the author's perspective and your own. Perhaps some of these views will strike a chord within you or give you a fresh perspective as to what success means to you.

PREFACE

When I was in high school in Southern California, the decisions of career choices were facing me as they do all teenagers. At that stage in life, the road ahead was clear and I could be anything I wanted to be. Still, my mind was filled with questions: What would I do with the rest of my life? How could I be successful? As I pondered these things, I realized that many people equated success with acquired wealth and possessions. But was that the only definition of success?

I have always believed that success is defined differently by each individual person and is shaped by values and beliefs, upbringing and environment. Even as a teenager, I wondered how people around the globe defined success and the ways in which their views affected their lives. As I grew up and found my career path, my interest in exploring these ideas strengthened. I began to travel to foreign countries and was surprised to discover there are as many definitions of success as there are people to give them.

What began as a young boy's search for a career eventually turned into a major project and the book you hold in your hands today. In 1995, I decided to pursue my objective to know how well-known successful people from every corner of the world defined success, and to share their views with others. After much thought and research, I began to compile a list of individuals to contact. I wanted it to be as diverse as possible and so I chose people from different parts of the world and all walks of life—from royalty to businesspeople and everything in between. I contacted individuals through in-person interviews, by phone and via letter. It was an exhaustive process, but exhilarating. I began receiving responses that confirmed my belief that success is a very individual, personal thing that may or may not be tied to material possessions.

It is my desire to give people the hope and inspiration they need to pursue their own path to success—to give them back the dreams they had as children to be and do whatever they want. As part of this project, I have also decided to help an organization that gives the dream back to children. The Make-A-Wish Foundation grants wishes to children under the age of 18 with life-threatening medical conditions. Part of the proceeds from this book are being donated to assist this marvelous organization in its efforts.

I hope you enjoy reading the responses of those who graciously participated in this project as much as I have enjoyed compiling and reading them myself.

ACKNOWLEDGMENTS

First and foremost, I wish to acknowledge all of the individuals who responded to my invitation to participate in this project. They made this book possible by providing their personal definitions of "success." Thank you for unselfishly taking the time to share your personal thoughts and for participating in our quest of "Giving Back the Dream™"! It is truly our hope that your insights will encourage those who read this book to continue in their own quest of personal fulfillment and success.

I would also like to acknowledge those who, although unable to participate at this time, responded with enthusiasm to our invitation. Thank you for taking the time to share your interest and good wishes. We hope to be able to include you in future editions of *Celebrating Success.*

I especially want to thank Peter Vegso and Gary Seidler at Health Communications who immediately recognized the benefits of publishing these contributions for you to enjoy.

Eric Smith and Heidi Brown, who unselfishly and liberally gave of their time, wisdom, insights and encouragement to this project. My many thanks to you both.

Susan Alison, who provided countless ideas, suggestions and ongoing enthusiasm throughout the project. Thanks, Susan.

Sue Grimsley at K.S. Grimsley Graphics for all of her support from the inception of this project to its completion. Her friendship and professionalism have been invaluable. Thank you, Sue.

Mike Akins and Jim Smart for the countless hours spent researching and inputting all of the information necessary to obtain the contributions. Thank you both for your dedication and commitment to the project.

Christine Belleris, my editor at Health Communications, who generously provided her assistance in bringing the pages of the manuscript to life. Thanks for all of your help, Christine.

And I would like to mention the following individuals who offered insights, valuable feedback and shared the vision of this book with me: Otto Smith, Corinne Harris, Mike Donlin, Julie Barnes, Roy Fell, Susan Bell, Angel Phelps, Mike Keyes, Jackie St. Germain, Richard Kelley, Debra Morris, Tracey Henson, Michael Ward and Jill Morales. My thanks to each of you.

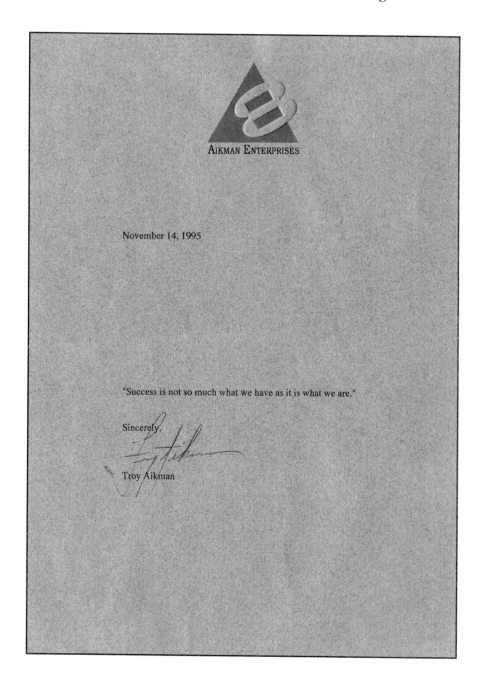

AIKMAN ENTERPRISES

November 14, 1995

"Success is not so much what we have as it is what we are."

Sincerely,

Troy Aikman

Troy Aikman
Professional Football Player

Erma Bombeck

Success is usually measured in terms of what we're remembered for. Keeping this in mind, I thought my kids would remember me as a woman who wrote twelve books, received sixteen honorary doctorates, and wrote for 31 million newspaper readers a week. My daughter told me that she would always remember me for caving in and buying her a stupid leather coat she thought she'd die if she didn't have...and ended up wearing once.

So you see, success isn't necessarily a monument to achievement, but small acts of love.

Erma Bombeck
Erma Bombeck

Erma Bombeck
Author/Columnist

F
O
R
T
Y
A
C
R
E
S
A
N
D
A
M
U
L
E
F
I
L
M
W
O
R
K
S
·
S
P
I
K
E
L
E
E

October 18, 1996

Dear Friends:

Filmmaking is a craft, and it can be learned like anything else; of course, it takes talent, but forget about it being something magical and mystical. Film is a powerful medium; it can influence how millions of people think, walk, talk, even live, plus you can make enormous sums of money. The idea is to keep the industry confined, let a small group of people have the control and make all the money. This is why one of my goals has been the demystification of film. I like to tell and show people it can be done. I'm saying don't fall for the junk like: You gotta be struck by lighting to be a filmmaker. To this end, I hope that what I've written about films and my films in general, has had a significant effect on people and the global collective consciousness.

Peace,

Spike Lee

YA-DIG
SHO-NUFF

Spike Lee
Motion Picture Director

Shannon Miller

I'm not sure I can define "success", but I can give you a few verses from the _Bible_ and from _Science and Health_ by Mary Baker Eddy on which I have relied frequently during the years to keep me on the right track:

"God is my strength and power and he maketh my way perfect"
                                    II Samuel 22:33

".. with God all things are possible"
                                    Matthew 19:26

"Hold thought to the enduring, the good, and the true and you will bring these into your experience proportionably to their occupancy of your thoughts."
                                    Mary Baker Eddy

"The feats of a gymnast prove that latent mental fears are subdued by him. The devotion of thought to an honest achievement makes the achievement possible."
                                    Mary Baker Eddy

While success means something a little different to each of us, we all enjoy the wonderful feeling of working hard trying our best to achieve an honest and reputable goal.
                                    Shannon Miller

Shannon Miller
Olympic Gold-Medal Gymnast

John Travolta

"ALL MY SUCCESS IS DUE TO SCIENTOLOGY, DIANETICS, AND THE STUDY OF THE WRITINGS OF L. RON HUBBARD."

John Travolta
Actor

ROBBINS RESEARCH INTERNATIONAL, INC.

I believe that the level of success we experience in life is in direct proportion to our commitment to the discipline of CANI! Constant and Never-Ending Improvement. It's only through continuous personal growth and unselfish contribution to others that one ever experiences the ultimate level of success known as fulfillment.

— Anthony Robbins

Anthony Robbins
Author/Motivational Speaker

Palace of Monaco,
July 9th, 1996.

In answer to your letter requesting my definition
of success, here is my way of seeing it:

"SUCCESS COMES TO THOSE WHO KNOW HOW TO WAIT"

Sincerely,

H.R.M. Prince Albert
Prince of Monaco

COSMOPOLITAN

Helen Gurley Brown, Editor · 224 West 57th Street, New York, New York, 10019, (212) 649-2000

June 10, 1996

This would be my definition of successful living:

1. You are happy a lot oftener than you are unhappy, although we all have down days.

2. You do some kind of work for which you get recognized and rewarded . . . it may even bring money but doesn't have to.

3. You make a few people happier just because you're here . . . successful living involves helping others with their problems and challenges.

4. You enjoy some things . . . it's different for each person . . . the things might be reading, sex, eating great stuff (as long as you don't get fat), talking to friends and loved ones, whatever special activity does it for you . . . for me it's dancing, along with the above.

All my best wishes,

Helen Gurley Brown

Helen Gurley Brown
Editor, *Cosmopolitan Magazine*

Imogene Coca

JUNE 26, 1996

SUCCESS IS BEING ABLE TO USE YOUR GIFTS. AS A LITTLE GIRL I WATCHED MY FATHER CONDUCT HIS ORCHESTRA NIGHT AFTER NIGHT AND IT WAS THERE THAT I FELL IN LOVE WITH THE THEATRE. IN MY PERSONAL LIFE SHARING WITH THE AUDIENCE, BOTH LAUGHTER AND TEARS, AND MANY TIMES MEETING WITH THEM BACKSTAGE AND KNOWING THAT WE HAVE TOUCHED EACH OTHERS LIVES — IT IS A FEELING THAT TRANSCENDS ANY WORDS. I AM VERY GRATEFUL.

Imogene Coca
Actress

Chris Evert
Professional Tennis Player

"Success Can Be measured by a bank account But the Value you hode for yourself is much more Rewarding"

Aug. 1996

Eartha Kitt

Eartha Kitt
Singer/Actress

Ann Landers
Chicago Tribune
435 North Michigan Avenue
Chicago, Illinois 60611

November 19, 1996

The best definition of success I have ever read was sent to me several years ago by Bessie Anderson Stanley. This definition sums up my thoughts perfectly. Here it is.

"He has achieved success who has lived well, laughed often and loved much; who has enjoyed the trust of pure women, the respect of intelligent men and the love of little children; who has filled his niche and accomplished his task; who has left the world better than he found it, whether by an improved poppy, a perfect poem, or a rescued soul; who has never lacked appreciation of earth's beauty, or failed to express it; who has always looked for the best in others and given them the best he had; whose life was an inspiration; whose memory a benediction."

Sincerely Yours,

Ann Landers

Ann Landers
Columnist/Author

"Let the mind soar"

Peter Max
Artist

RENÉ RUSSO

Wisdom is better than
Rubies or Pearls
Or <u>anything</u> you could
wish for. ☺ proverbs
8:11

René Russo
Actress

FRANCESCO SCAVULLO, INC.

June 3, 1996

    I cannot think of the right word to explain the incredible feeling deep in my heart every time someone stops me on the street and says, "Mr. Scavullo thank you for all the beautiful photographs you have taken. They bring me great joy!"

    The word, I guess, is joy. My career as a photographer has brought me great joy.

Love,

Francesco Scavullo

Francesco Scavullo

Francesco Scavullo
Photographer

Peter Vidmar

I believe that success is the inner peace that comes from knowing your daily behavior is in line with the most important things in your life. That doesn't mean that everything we do will be fun, exciting, or easy. In many cases we will experience just the opposite, but we are willing to make those sacrifices, and pay the price that needs to be paid to arrive at something we feel is of great worth to us.

I was fortunate to surround myself with people whom I considered the best in my sport. They were extremely diligent, not just on the good days, when they felt good and got instant results, but more importantly they knew how to focus on the bad days, when they were tired, when the results didn't come immediately. I knew if I could become like those great gymnasts, I might become one myself!

Peter Vidmar

2 Golds, 1 Silver
1984 Olympics

Peter Vidmar
Olympic Gold-Medal Gymnast

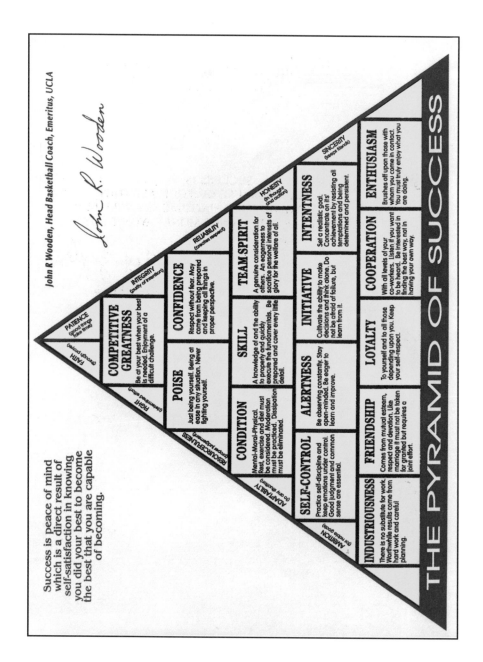

John R Wooden, Head Basketball Coach, Emeritus, UCLA

John R. Wooden

Success is peace of mind which is a direct result of self-satisfaction in knowing you did your best to become the best that you are capable of becoming.

THE PYRAMID OF SUCCESS

FAITH (through prayer)

PATIENCE (good things take time)

INTEGRITY (purity of intention)

RELIABILITY (creates respect)

HONESTY (in thought and action)

SINCERITY (keeps friends)

COMPETITIVE GREATNESS
Be at your best when your best is needed. Enjoyment of a difficult challenge.

CONFIDENCE
Respect without fear. May come from being prepared and keeping all things in proper perspective.

TEAM SPIRIT
A genuine consideration for others. An eagerness to sacrifice personal interests of glory for the welfare of all.

ENTHUSIASM
Brushes off upon those with whom you come in contact. You must truly enjoy what you are doing.

FIGHT (determined effort)

POISE
Just being yourself. Being at ease in any situation. Never fighting yourself.

SKILL
A knowledge of and the ability to properly and quickly execute the fundamentals. Be prepared and cover every little detail.

INITIATIVE
Cultivate the ability to make decisions and think alone. Do not be afraid of failure, but learn from it.

INTENTNESS
Set a realistic goal. Concentrate on its' achievement by resisting all temptations and being determined and persistent.

RESOURCEFULNESS (proper judgement)

CONDITION
Mental-Moral-Physical. Rest, exercise and diet must be considered. Moderation must be practiced. Dissipation must be eliminated.

ALERTNESS
Be observing constantly. Stay open-minded. Be eager to learn and improve.

LOYALTY
To yourself and to all those depending upon you. Keep your self-respect.

COOPERATION
With all levels of your co-workers. Listen if you want to be heard. Be interested in finding the best way, not in having your own way.

ADAPTABILITY (to any situation)

SELF-CONTROL
Practice self-discipline and keep emotions under control. Good judgment and common sense are essential.

FRIENDSHIP
Comes from mutual esteem, respect and devotion. Like marriage it must not be taken for granted but requires a joint effort.

AMBITION (for noble goals)

INDUSTRIOUSNESS
There is no substitute for work. Worthwhile results come from hard work and careful planning.

John R. Wooden
Head Basketball Coach Emeritus,
University of California, Los Angeles

The Zig Ziglar Corporation

THE TRAINING COMPANY

Zig Ziglar
Chairman

SUCCESS IS
THE MAXIMUM USE OF YOUR ABILITIES
TO GET MORE OF THE THINGS MONEY WILL BUY
AND ALL OF THE THINGS MONEY WON'T BUY.

Zig Ziglar

ZIG ZIGLAR

Zig Ziglar
Author/Motivational Speaker

WALLY AMOS
'THE COOKIE MAN'

THE UNCLE
NONAME
COOKIE
COMPANY

"TURN LEMONS
INTO LEMONADE"

SUCCESS IS DOING WHAT YOU LOVE TO DO, WITH PEOPLE THAT YOU LOVE, IN AN ENVIRONMENT THAT YOU LOVE.

Wally A

WALLY AMOS

Wally Amos
Founder, Famous Amos Cookies and The No Name Cookie Company

BEN NIGHTHORSE CAMPBELL
COLORADO

United States Senate
WASHINGTON, DC 20510-0605

December 14, 1995

Thank you for asking me my definition of success for your publication. I hope your endeavor can bring a little hope to those who read your publication when it is finished.

The feeling of success for me is riding the Harley with the cool wind blowing through my hair and a sense of freedom all around me. However, since this is perhaps not a tangible definition of success that many people can draw from, I would like to offer up a poem that I think best defines success. The poem is called *Success is...* by Henry Emerson Fosdick.

Success is...

To laugh often and much
To win the respect of intelligent people
and the affection of children;
To earn the appreciation of honest
critics and endure the betrayal of
false friends;
To appreciate beauty;
To find the best in others;
To leave the world a bit better, whether
by a healthy child, a garden patch or
a redeemed social condition;
To know even one life has breathed
easier because you lived.
This is to have succeeded.

I appreciate you including me on your list of individuals to contribute to your project. I hope this can help in some way.

Sincerely,

Ben Nighthorse Campbell

1129 PENNSYLVANIA STREET   19 OLD TOWN SQUARE   743 HORIZON CT.   105 E. VERMIJO   835 E. 2nd AVENUE   720 N. MAIN STREET
DENVER, CO 80203   SUITE 238, #33   SUITE 386   SUITE 600   SUITE 228   SUITE 402
303/866-1900   FT. COLLINS, CO 80524   GRAND JUNCTION, CO 81506   COLORADO SPRINGS, CO 80903   DURANGO, CO 81301   PUEBLO, CO 81003
303/224-1909   303/241-6631   719/636-9092   303/247-1609   719/542-6987

PRINTED ON RECYCLED PAPER

Ben Nighthorse Campbell
U.S. Senator from Colorado

DAVID CARUSO

KNOW WHAT YOU KNOW
AND LIVE WITH IT

David

David Caruso
Actor

B O B   K A N E

HOLLYWOOD
CALIFORNIA

1

<u>SUCCESS</u>
<u>THE BOB KANE STORY</u>

It is my belief that every success story that I have researched began with a <u>dream</u> as did mine. Furthermore, all human beings are given the gift by life to discover their own personal unique <u>innate</u> <u>creative</u> <u>potential</u>, no matter how big or small, use it to the utmost degree in order to fulfill themselves and evolve into a state of inner peace, fulfillment and success.

The story of Batman is also my life story. In this great country there are many Horatio Alger rags-to-riches tales - mine is one of them. The American Dream can be obtained by most anyone with ambition who is willing to strive for it. What one needs is the desire and ability to reach for the stars, along with the tenacity, perception and perseverance to attain this lofty goal.

The German author and philosopher Goethe had this to say on becoming a success in life. I quote:

Until one is committed, there is
hesitancy, the chance to draw back,
always ineffectiveness. Concerning
all acts of initiative [and creation]
there is one elementary truth the
ignorance of which kills countless
ideas and splendid plans:

That moment one definitely
commits oneself, then
providence moves too...

Whatever you can do or dream you
can, begin it. Boldness has genius,
power and magic in it.

Begin it *now!*

This profound advice sums up the philosophy which I aspired to at the beginning of my cartooning career when I was a fledgling "doodler" living in a poor neighborhood in the Bronx. I intuitively knew what I wanted out of life by adhering to my innate creative potential, set my vocational goals and, despite early setbacks, followed them through to their fruition. Batman grew from a tiny acorn to become a mighty icon in my lifetime. How gratifying!

Bob Kane
Cartoonist (Batman)

BOB KANE
HOLLYWOOD
CALIFORNIA

2

Of course, Destiny and Providence do play a major part in one's life; being at the right place at the right time helps immensely. Mine was the budding innovative comic book industry that began during the mid-30's, while I was still in my teens.

However, one has to possess enough foresight to grasp the opportunity when it presents itself, otherwise the right door will open and close - which could make the difference between success and failure in your chosen career.

Fortunately, I recognized Lady Luck early in life, when "She" smiled upon me, and I have been having a successful courtship with her ever since. Remember to follow your dream... everything is possible for those who believe!

Bob Kane
Cartoonist (Batman)

Tom Landry
Dallas, Texas

December 20, 1995

Definition of Success:

True Success comes when your priorities are in
the right order -- God first, Family second and
Football third.

Tom Landry

Tom Landry
Dallas Cowboys Football Coach

Chicken Soup for the **Soul**

#1 New York Times
B E S T S E L L E R

Jack Canfield
Mark Victor Hansen
Authors

December 11, 1996

I believe that everybody's definition of success is different. In my mind, to be successful, you have to discover your unique life purpose, diligently follow your heart and stubbornly pursue that which most excites you with unflagging enthusiasm and perseverance.

I have enjoyed a great deal of fame and fortune in my life, but that is not what has brought me the greatest pleasure and fulfillment. For me, I have felt most successful when I am inspiring and empowering people to love and accept themselves more deeply, to open their hearts to others more fully, to trust and believe in themselves more completely, and to pursue their dreams more boldly and passionately. Knowing I can make this kind of a difference in the lives of others is what most deeply motivates me.

I have found that I can do this through many channels—books, tapes, seminars, radio, television, syndicated columns, speeches, one-on-one mentoring, group coaching sessions, parenting, managing and delivering trainings. The hundreds of letters I receive each week from people who tell me that our work has changed their lives makes all the late nights and hard work worth it.

I also feel successful when I walk the talk that I share with others. When Mark Victor Hansen and I decided to write the first **Chicken Soup for the Soul** book, very few people believed in the project. The book was rejected by over 30 publishers, but we hung in there for two years and never gave up because in our hearts we knew that there was a deep need for positive, uplifting, inspirational stories in the world. Three years later, there are over 11 million copies of our books in print in 23 languages! The number of people who have read the books and been changed by them helps me to feel successful at a very deep level.

I feel grateful to have had the opportunity to express myself so fully while doing what I love and knowing that it has touched the lives of millions of people worldwide.

Jack Canfield
Co-author, **Chicken Soup for the Soul**

Jack Canfield
Author/Motivational Speaker

Ernest **Orlando** **Lawrence**
Berkeley **National** **Laboratory**

Office of the Associate Director-at-Large
Glenn T. Seaborg

My Secret to Success

by

Glenn T. Seaborg

The most important secret to success is simple hard work. Many a person of only better-than-average ability has accomplished, just on the basis of work and perseverance, much greater things than some geniuses. Such a hardworking individual will succeed where a lazy genius may fail. Some scientific discoveries are made by armchair research, but most of them require considerable experimental work and represent a lot of perseverance and perspiration, as well as a properly conceived method of attack. You will have to evaluate your own characteristics and try to place yourself in the environment most likely, as a routine result, to draw hard work from you in order to succeed.

Operated by the University of California for the United States Department of Energy

Glenn T. Seaborg
Nobel Prize in Chemistry Laureate

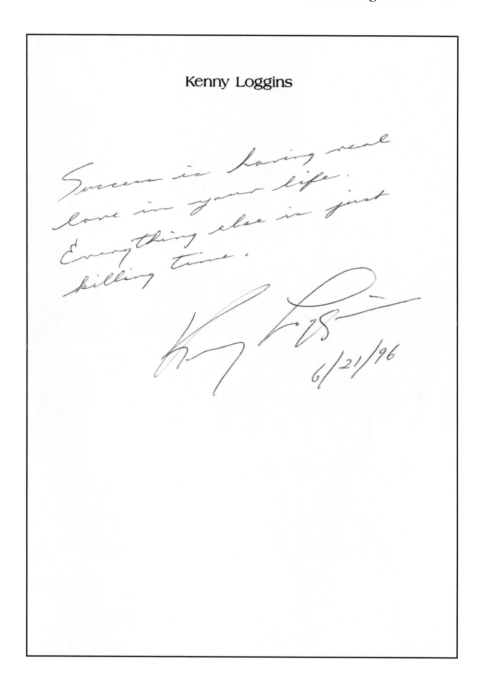

Kenny Loggins

Success is having real love in your life. Everything else is just killing time.

6/21/96

Kenny Loggins
Singer/Songwriter

ED McMAHON

November 6, 1995

"SUCCESS" what a great word! What a great concept to be desired!

My idea of success is that it is the reward for hard work. My father was a very practical man, and he said: "Son never go after money or fame, just be a success in your field of endeavor and everything else will follow."

What a visionary he turned out to be!

The money and fame are wonderful to enjoy, but the best part of it all is to fulfill your goals in your chosen field of endeavor. Even if your lot in life is not necessarily the one you'd choose. Hard work at what ever you do is its own reward which is *"SUCCESS."*

Cordially,

Ed McMahon

Ed McMahon
Television Personality

WENDY'S INTERNATIONAL, INC.

R. DAVID THOMAS
Senior Chairman of the Board & Founder

Success

There are all kinds of success and all kinds of ways to achieve it. I know bus drivers who are as successful as bankers, anonymous computer programmers who are more successful than some of the biggest sports celebrities. I also know glamorous Hollywood stars who are failures because they let their egos get in the way of everything else.

Sometimes you can spot true success. Sometimes you can't. Success can take many forms, but one thing's for sure: the ingredients of success are basically the same for everyone.

Success is about living a life honestly and with integrity. Here are a few "secrets" I learned along the way:

Learning from your mistakes is never fun, but that seems to be where you'll get the best education. I've learned plenty of things "the hard way."

Nothing worthwhile is accomplished without hard work and total commitment.

Taking risks is vital to personal and professional growth . . . but don't forget to enjoy the rewards of your accomplishments.

Success means nothing if you don't give back to the community - - it's your right and your responsibility.

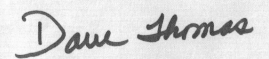

Dave Thomas
Founder, Wendy's International

I believe that a successful life is measured not in wealth or power, but in effective service to one's fellow man. This is easier said than done, of course, as it requires the vision of a brighter tomorrow, the patience and determination to perservere when the future looks grim, and the courage to stay the course in the face of adversity.

Let me relate some wisdom which my grandfather, the founder of this kingdom, imparted to me when I was a young man. He told me that he perceived his life as a link in a continuous chain of those who served our nation, and that he expected me to be a new and strong link in the same chain. I have recalled this statement over and over again, and have remembered its intent more than any other. To shoulder our responsibilities to the family, to the community, to the nation and to our fellow man—indeed, to bestow upon future generations the birthright of a better world—is the noblest calling and the hallmark of a successful life.

Hussein I

H.M. King Hussein I
King of Jordan

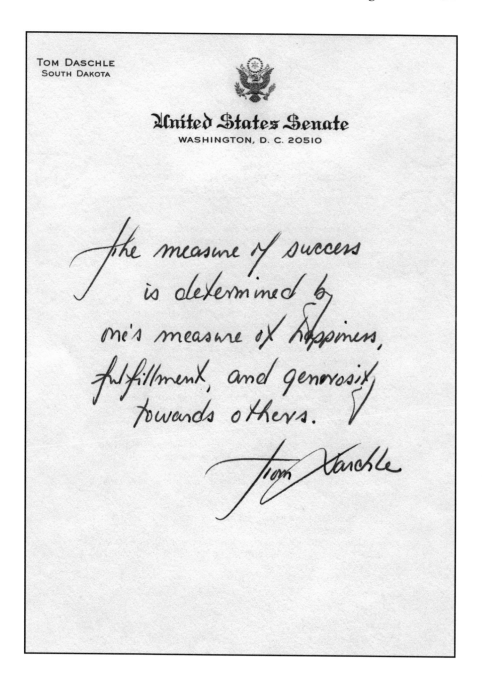

TOM DASCHLE
SOUTH DAKOTA

𝔘nited 𝔖tates 𝔖enate
WASHINGTON, D. C. 20510

*The measure of success
is determined by
one's measure of happiness,
fulfillment, and generosity
towards others.*

Tom Daschle

Tom Daschle
U.S. Senator from South Dakota

THE PRESIDENT OF MALTA

~ A DEFINITION OF SUCCESS ~
MESSAGE
by
HIS EXCELLENCY DR. UGO MIFSUD BONNICI
PRESIDENT OF MALTA

There are as many definitions of success as there are human beings. The realization of success is not only relative but also subjective. 'Life depends upon the liver' as they say in that famous pun. Everyone in the world tends to measure one's attainments against one's aspirations or the expectations of the society in which one lives.

Generally speaking, success is the state of having achieved, of having reached one's goals, of having attained a climactical state of harmony between one's soul and one's body, one's past and one's present, one's self and the milieu in which one lives. In fact we tend to equate failure (as against success), with a <u>split</u> personality, with being a <u>misfit</u>, a <u>maladjusted</u> person.

Generally speaking, however, a successful person is one who is at peace with oneself in the sense that one bears no grudge against one's tribe, one's family, one's surroundings and one's self - actually a person who is well attuned to the circumstances of one's existence.

Self-fulfilment sought through the pursuance of shallow and frivolous goals is a partial palliative to the essentially spiritual void in all of us.

Equilibrium can only be brought about on a personal level through spiritual (as against material) pursuits.

Religion, philosophical enquiry, the contemplation of beauty, poetry, art, music, the intercourse with nature, yoga - call it what you will - all these add to life the indispensable dimension which makes it worth living and which gives man the truly divine attribute of making him 'the measure of all things'.

UGO MIFSUD BONNICI
President of Malta

11 May, 1996.

Ugo Mifsud Bonnici
President of Malta

Cathy Lee Crosby

Your life is God's gift to you;
Your success is your gift back.

-CLC

You can compromise without compromising yourself.
You can change without losing your uniqueness.
You can grow without growing apart.
You can give without losing anything.
You can open up without being judged.
You can disagree without arguing.
You can feel without losing control.
You can keep the passion alive in a long-term relationship.
You can be mature without losing the child inside of you.

You cannot be known unless you open your heart.
You cannot love without being vulnerable.
You cannot be intimate without taking a risk.
You cannot share feelings in a non-supportive environment.
You cannot enter a relationship demanding a guarantee.
You cannot be interdependent unless you're first independent.
You cannot be controlling and spontaneous at the same time.
You cannot be alive without making mistakes.
You cannot realize your dreams if you don't have well defined goals.
You cannot grow unless you learn from your mistakes.
You cannot forgive another until you've forgiven yourself first.
You cannot heal a broken heart until you risk it again.

-Gospel according to Godek, Revisited

Cathy Lee Crosby
Television Personality

FREDERICK K.C. PRICE, Ph.D.
Founder and Pastor

"Success is ascertaining from God's master success manual, the Bible, what His plan and purpose is for man on earth; then, by applying the principles found therein to my life, success is the natural outcome of that pursuit."

Frederick K.C. Price, Ph.D.

Frederick K. C. Price
Religious Leader

PAT BOONE
■ ENTERPRISES June 6, 1996

Here's my quote for your book:

> "By all accounts, the wisest man
> who ever lived was King Solomon.
> He was the richest, most powerful,
> most famous and revered mortal man
> who ever lived. Perhaps he might
> have something to tell us about
> genuine success.
>
> Indeed, he does.
>
> At the end of the Book of Ecclesiastes,
> which he authored, he makes this
> profound and conclusive statement:
>
> > **Now all have been heard;**
> > **Here is the conclusion of the matter:**
> > **Fear God and keep His commandments,**
> > **for this is the whole duty of man.**
> > **For God will bring every deed into**
> > > **judgment,**
> > **including every hidden thing, whether**
> > > **it is good or evil.**
> > (Ecc.12:13-14)
>
> Fearing God and keeping His commandments,
> to the best of our abilities, is our whole
> duty in life. Failure in this vital area
> makes material accomplishment meaningless;
> success in performing these duties
> transcends any material consideration.
>
> So, for me, the only reward or token
> of success in my whole existence will
> be His words, "Well done, good and
> faithful servant. Enter into the
> joys of your Lord".

That will be success.

Warmly,

Pat Boone

Pat Boone
Singer/Actor

Bill Conti

Success is Definitely Not A Destination.

Bill Conti [signature]

Bill Conti
Composer

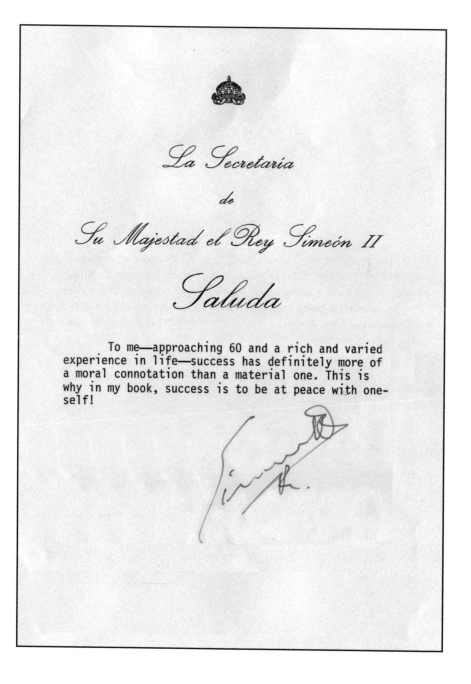

La Secretaría

de

Su Majestad el Rey Simeón II

Saluda

To me—approaching 60 and a rich and varied experience in life—success has definitely more of a moral connotation than a material one. This is why in my book, success is to be at peace with one-self!

H.M. Rey Simeón II
King of Bulgaria

LeVar Burton

Success for me is all about being in alignment with what I know to be my true life's purpose. This is the only barometer I need in deciding whether or not I am succeeding as a husband. or father, or in my career.

My reason for being here is to advance God as best as I am able, with every resource at my disposal. When I live my life from that perspective, I can't help but succeed.

LeVar Burton

LeVar Burton
Actor

Brenda Lee

Join the great company of those who make barren places of life fruitful with kindness. Carry a vision of heaven in your souls and you shall make the world correspond to that vision.

External conditions are the accidents of life, its outer trappings. The great enduring realities are love of service. Joy is the holy fire that keeps our purpose warm and our intelligence aglow. Resolve to keep happy and your joy and you shall form an invincible host against difficulty.

This is a quote from Helen Keller that I have drawn inspiration from. Hope you find it inspiring too.

Sincerely,

Brenda Lee

Brenda Lee
Singer

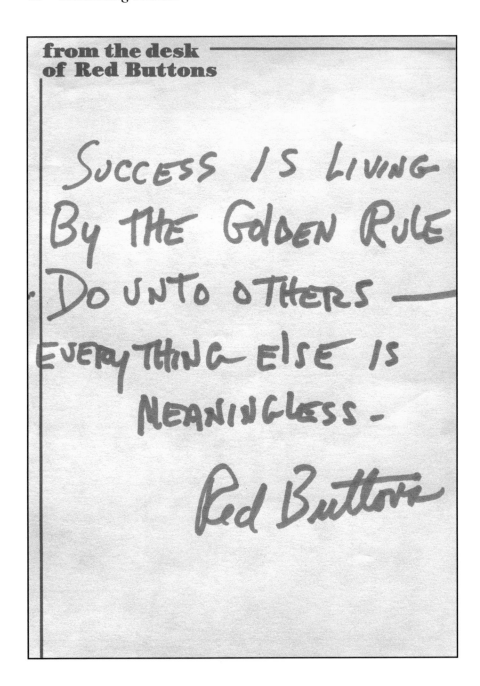

from the desk of Red Buttons

SUCCESS IS LIVING
By THE GOLDEN RULE
DO UNTO OTHERS —
EVERYTHING ELSE IS
NEANINGLESS.

Red Buttons

Red Buttons
Actor

Success is drinking a lot of water every day —
Walter Matthau

Walter Matthau
Actor

June 11, 96

Happiness to me is one's ability to be his or her very best at whatever their chosen profession or job may be. It's at that time you can look into the mirror and like what you see. The definition of success varies with each individual and the end result is again back to that individual. I view a person can be successful in being an excellent gardener as well a corporate v.p. or a poet. Once again it's how each one of us view ourselves! If we are happy I think you will find that the individual is also successful in whatever they're doing, from being a mother to the president of the United States.

Most sincerely,

Bud Yorkin

Bud Yorkin
Motion Picture Producer

Mary Ann Mobley Collins

Success may be defined in many different ways. Often it is attributed to the amount of money one is able to obtain in a lifetime. To others, it is fame. However, I believe a poem by Ralph Waldo Emerson most accurately defines my definition of success, and one which we all can achieve.

SUCCESS

To laugh often and much; to win the respect
of intelligent people and affection of children;
to earn the appreciation of honest critics and
endure the betrayal of false friends; to appreciate
beauty, to find the best in others; to leave the
world a bit better, whether by a healthy child, a
garden patch or a redeemed social condition; to know
even one life has breathed easier because you have
lived. This is to have succeeded.

-- Ralph Waldo Emerson

Mary Ann Mobley Collins
Actress/Miss America

GlaxoWellcome

Gertrude B. Elion, D.Sc.

June 11, 1996

You have asked for my definition of success. As a scientist engaged in pharmaceutical research for my entire career of more than 50 years, success means discovering new drugs which can alleviate human suffering and save lives.

I have had the unmatched thrill of synthesizing and developing a drug which helps to cure childhood leukemia. My colleagues and I also developed a drug which made possible kidney transplantation from unrelated donors by preventing rejection of the transplanted organ. In addition, we discovered drugs to treat gout and several different kinds of herpes virus infections.

When I received the Nobel Prize in Physiology or Medicine in 1988, many people asked me whether that wasn't what I had aimed for all my life. Of course, it was not. One doesn't think about that kind of recognition as a goal. It's obviously very exciting and gratifying to get such as award. However, the true measure of success lies in developing medicines which improve people's health and longevity.

Being a research scientist has made it possible for me to have not only a very enjoyable life, but one which has also benefited others.

Sincerely,

Gertrude B. Elion

Gertrude B. Elion, D. Sc.

Gertrude B. Elion
Nobel Prize in Physiology or Medicine Laureate

HARVARD UNIVERSITY

N. Bloembergen
Professor, Emeritus

Division of Applied Sciences and Department of Physics

June 12, 1996

"At any stage in your life, set for yourself a goal that will not harm others and always do your best in trying to reach that goal."

Sincerely,

N. Bloembergen

N. Bloembergen

N. Bloembergen
Nobel Prize in Physics Laureate

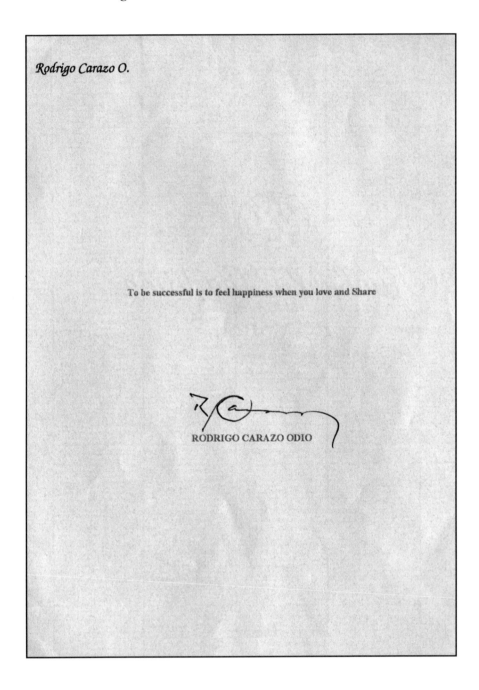

Rodrigo Carazo O.

To be successful is to feel happiness when you love and Share

RODRIGO CARAZO ODIO

Rodrigo Carazo Odio
President of Costa Rica

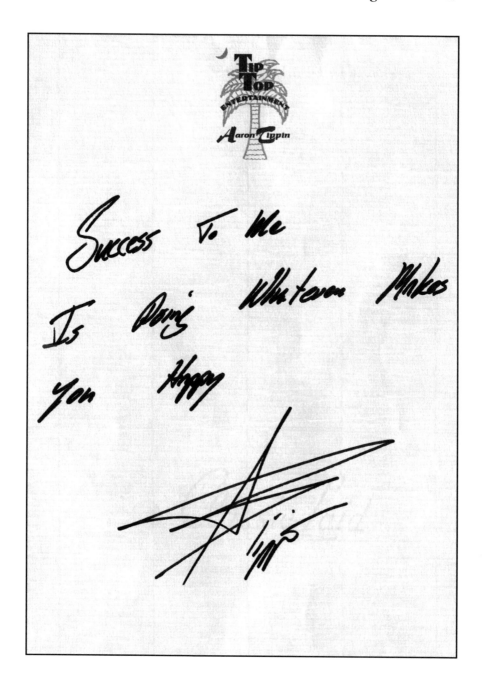

Success To Me
Its Doing Whatever Makes
You Happy

Aaron Tippin
Singer

WHAT IS SUCCESS?

Having children and keeping them alive until they're 21.

WHAT IS MORE SUCCESSFUL?

Having children that want to be friends and hang out with you when they're grown up.

WHAT IS SUCCESS?

Finding something you are passionate about in your lifetime.

WHAT IS MORE SUCCESSFUL?

Getting paid to do it.

MORE SUCCESSFUL?

Getting paid a lot to do it.

WHAT IS SUCCESS?

Being at peace with God.

MORE SUCCESSFUL?

Being at peace with your fellow man.

MORE SUCCESSFUL?

Being at peace with your enemies.

Victoria Jackson
Actress/Comedienne

WHAT IS SUCCESS?

Achieving a goal.

MORE SUCCESSFUL?

Achieving a goal with sincere humility.

WHAT IS SUCCESS?

Collecting a group of friends and family that love you and make you laugh.

MORE SUCCESSFUL?

Giving a group of friends and family love and making them laugh.

MORE SUCCESSFUL?

Being patient and kind to the rude, ignorant, and completely unhelpful stranger on the phone.

by Victoria Jackson

June II, 1996

Victoria Jackson
Actress/Comedienne

DEPARTMENT OF VETERANS AFFAIRS

June 11, 1996

This is a quote at the giving of the Nobel Prize in Physiology or Medicine in 1977.

"Rosalyn Yalow's name is forever associated with her methodology of measuring the presence of hormones in the blood at concentrations as low as one thousand billionths of a gram per milliliter of blood. This was a necessity, since a great many hormones, primarily the so-called protein hormones, are present in the blood in such small quantities. Before Yalow, these hormones could not be determined quantitatively in the blood, and therefore, active research in this field had stagnated."

"As a result of mixing in a test tube a known quantity of radioactive insulin with a known quantity of antibodies against insulin, a specific amount of the insulin becomes attached to these antibodies. Subsequently, if one adds to this mixture a small amount of blood which contains insulin, the insulin of the blood becomes similarly attached to the antibodies and a certain portion of the radioactive insulin is detached from the antibodies. The higher the concentration of insulin is in the blood sample, the larger is the amount of radioactive insulin that will be detached from the antibodies. The amount of radioactive insulin thus removed can easily be determined, providing an exact measure of the amount of insulin present in the blood sample."

These statements from the speech by Professor Rolf Luft bring memories of the presentation to me of the Nobel Prize for Physiology or Medicine.

Sincerely yours,

Rosalyn S. Yalow, Ph.D.
Senior Medical Investigator Emeritus, VA
Solomon A. Berson Distinguished Professor-at-Large
Mount Sinai School of Medicine, CUNY
Nobel Laureate in Physiology or Medicine, 1977

Rosalyn S. Yalow
Nobel Prize in Physiology or Medicine Laureate

June 13, 1996

There are two - and maybe three - definitions of success. The first is the realization of one's personal desires and ambitions. The second is the achievement of certain goals which others might have expected of, or wished for, you. And third, success is measured as such by alien standards of others. For example, one who has made a fortune might be called "successful" but that same person might well consider material wealth not nearly as gratifying as spiritual or intellectual wealth.

In short, there are many definitions, interpretations and standards of success. One would have been to write a satisfactory reply to your letter. In my view, I have <u>not</u> succeeded!

Good luck is the wish of

yours sincerely,

Douglas Fairbanks, Jr.

Douglas Fairbanks, Jr.
Actor

PURDUE UNIVERSITY

HERBERT C. BROWN

MY SUCCESS —
The Discovery and Exploration of a New Continent of Chemistry

In 1992 we celebrated the 500th anniversary of the discovery of America. We now know the geography of the Earth sufficiently well to make it clear that there remain no new Physical Continents to be discovered. But there remain many new Continents of Knowledge awaiting discovery and exploration by energetic and enthusiastic explorers. In the past sixty years my students and I have discovered and explored such a new Continent, the Borane Continent, a discovery which led to the awarding of the Nobel Prize in Chemistry in 1979.

In 1936 I was graduating from the University of Chicago with the B.S. degree. My classmate, Sarah Baylen, gave me a graduation present, a book by Alfred Stock, "The Hydrides of Boron and Silicon", Cornell University Press, Ithaca, N.Y., 1933. This book kindled my interest in the hydrides of boron, so I decided to do my doctorate work on these little-explored materials. Why did Sarah select this book for me out of the hundreds of chemistry books available in the University Bookstore? This was the time of the Great Depression. None of us had much money. This was the cheapest chemistry book available ($2.00 plus $0.06 sales tax). This then is one way to find a new, rich field of research that can lead to the Nobel!

In sixty years of study we have made major contributions to the development of new synthetic methods based on diborane and its derivatives—the Borane Continent. Among the recognitions I have received may be mentioned: election to the National Academy of Sciences, 1957; the National Medal of Science, 1969; the Nobel Prize in Chemistry, 1979; the Priestley Medal of the American Chemical Society, 1981; the National Academy of Science Award in Chemical Sciences, 1987; and the Japanese Decoration, Order of the Rising Sun and Gold and Silver Star, 1989.

Finally, my classmate, who started it all, has been my wife for 59 years.

Both my wife and I had lost our fathers to illnesses at an early age. Life was difficult for fatherless families in the pre-Social Security age. We met at Crane Junior College in 1932, the only college in the city of Chicago which did not charge tuition. But by working with energy and optimism, we achieved both scientific and financial success, and a wonderful life together.

Herbert C. Brown

Herbert C. Brown
Nobel Prize in Chemistry Laureate

STATE OF DELAWARE
OFFICE OF THE GOVERNOR

THOMAS R. CARPER
GOVERNOR

December 15, 1995

Thank you for the opportunity to provide a few words of wisdom to benefit the Make - A - Wish Foundation. I am pleased to share my four "rules for living," derived from family teachings and my own life experience:

1. Do what is right;
2. Do your best;
3. Treat others as you would have them treat you; and
4. Never, never give up.

These principles guide the decisions I make each and every day as governor of the State of Delaware. They have served me well in my life and I hope will be useful to others.

Best wishes to you in your endeavor.

Sincerely,

Thomas R. Carper
Governor

TATNALL BUILDING
DOVER, DELAWARE 19901
(302) 739 - 4101
FAX (302) 739 - 2775

CARVEL STATE OFFICE BLDG.
WILMINGTON, DELAWARE 19801
(302) 577 - 3210
FAX (302) 577 - 3118

Thomas R. Carper
Governor of Delaware

FROM THE HOTEL BED OF
PAULA POUNDSTONE

I HAVE NEVER BEEN SUCCESSFUL, EXACTLY.
I WISH I COULD TELL YOU THAT
I NEVER CARED ABOUT THAT SORT
OF THING. I HAVE, THOUGH. IN SOME
WAYS, CLASSIC SUCCESS GAVE UP ON
ME BEFORE I GAVE UP ON IT
(THE BIG STAR, BIG MONEY KIND).
    IF I COULD GO TO BED EVERY
NIGHT KNOWING THAT, if I DIDN'T MAKE
THE WORLD BETTER THAT DAY, AT LEAST
I DIDN'T MAKE IT WORSE, I'D
BE SUCCESSFUL BEYOND MY WILDEST
        DREAMS.
    I WOULD ALSO LIKE TO VACUUM THE WHOLE
HOUSE.
                        PAULA POUNDST...

Paula Poundstone
Comedienne

norm crosby

June 17, 1996

One of the main reasons that people hesitate to act —
to vote, to complain, to speak out against an
injustice or even to try something new or contrary
in their usual routines— is because they do not
honestly feel that they would make a difference.

For several years I have been a National Cohost on
the MDA Jerry Lewis Telethon and I am currently in
my twelfth year as Ambassador of Goodwill for the
world famous City of Hope Hospital and research
Center.

Both facilities depend entirely, as do most of our
charitable organizations, on individual contributions
to maintain their multi-million dollar budgets each
year.

Imagine, if every person should suddenly decide
that his or her contribution was not important.
Our entire system of fundraising for so many
worthy causes would totally collapse.

I believe that the following quote will answer any
doubts that anyone might have about taking any action
which may, at first, seem futile or even impossible.
I do not remember where I read the lines, but I have
never forgotten them.

"I am only one, but still I am one.
I cannot do everything, but still I can do something.
And because I cannot do everything, I must not refuse
to do the something that I can do."

With all good wishes,

Norm Crosby
Norm Crosby

Norm Crosby
Comedian

Joan van Ark

When I was growing up in Boulder, Colorado, my bedroom wall had quotes that 'spoke' to me...and inspired me as I struggled with my homework.

With a tiny one-word edit, this one comes to mind:

Success
~~Luck~~ is what happens when preparation meets opportunity.

...and my own addiction:

never - EVER give up!

— *Joan van Ark*

Joan van Ark
Actress

Success in any career or profession is that which brings each individual the most personal satisfaction. It is NOT money, fame or recognition. It is knowing that you do the very best you can, EVERY DAY.

As for an experience that greatly influenced me, I like to cite the journey I made to Florida to see and gain some inspiration from a childhood role model, Ding Darling. I grew up in Des Moines where his cartoons appeared daily in the Register and Tribune newspaper, often on the front page. He was an arch conservative of the 30's and 40's.

Darling was retired and living in the Florida Keys and I finally was able to get some of his time. I showed him my portfolio of cartoons from the University of Iowa Daily Iowan, where I began my cartooning career. After a cursory look, he gave my cartoons back to me and said "Get into another line of work."

I already had a job at The Denver Post, and I think that inspired me to try to prove him wrong. If anything, it made me research issues deeper, prepare to defend each of my stands, and further, and always, to read, read, read.

I did go on to win a Pulitzer Prize while I was at The Denver Post, and two more while drawing for The Los Angeles Times.

Incidentally, Darling was totally correct in his assessment. At that time, my cartoons were shallow, full of labels, and had very little impact except that some of them were funny. I have devoted my career to changing all those traits. And, I tell this story to many aspiring cartoonists who now come to me for critique.

Paul Conrad

Paul Conrad
Editorial Cartoonist

BAYLOR COLLEGE OF MEDICINE

OFFICE OF THE CHANCELLOR

In response to your request for my definition for success based on my own experience, I am sending you this bit of my personal philosophy:

I have found that the road to success is paved with self-discipline, industry, and perseverance. My life and work have been guided largely by an appreciation for order and beauty in the universe, reverence for life, and compassion for suffering humanity. The desire, instilled in me by my parents, to make a contribution to human welfare during my sojourn on earth has motivated me to do my utmost to help others preserve life and lift it to the highest level of health, happiness, and personal fulfillment.

I believe that one should always strive for excellence, and turn all adversities into successes.

Kind personal regards.

Sincerely,

Michael E. DeBakey, M. D.

Michael E. DeBakey
Heart Surgeon

RICHARD ADLER

MY DEFINITION OF TRUE SUCCESS

What is <u>true</u> success? To me it is not amassing a great fortune or being a famous person. To me, <u>true</u> success can be measured by a certain feeling I sometimes get...a kind of glow (or warmth). Sometimes, when I have just completed a work -- a song, a symphonic suite, a ballet, a children's book -- and when that work resonates deep inside my soul I feel inordinately successful. Even when the work doesn't find itself out there in the marketplace as a winner on the best-selling charts, I still have it -- that assured knowledge of having achieved true success. It is then that I know I have measured up to the best. That is the ingredient that makes hard work really worthwhile. That is the only payoff I need.

Robert Browning, in his great epic poem "Andrea del Sarto, The Faultless Painter" declares "Ah, but the reach exceeds the grasp." Striving and striving the utmost is a signpost along the true success highway. I often ask myself why do I still write when I no longer have to? The answer is always the same. I write because I have to...because it is my passion to compose -- because there is no other way I can find true pleasure. There is nothing else I can do but write and write. This is my yardstick for measuring true success. Therefore, experiencing true pleasure means finding true success.

Richard Adler

Richard Adler
Composer/Lyricist

December, 1995

Dear Neighbors,

It was interesting to know about the work of The Institute
for Successful Living. It's an honor to be included in this
project, and I'm happy to share my thoughts and feelings
about success with you. What it takes to be successful in
what you do is much the same, no matter where you live, what
school you attend, or what kind of work you do. To me, what
makes someone successful is managing a healthy combination
of wishing and doing. Wishing doesn't make anything happen,
but it certainly can be the start of some important
happenings. I hope you'll feel good enough about yourself
that you'll continue to wish and dream. And, that you'll do
all you can to help the best of your wishes come true.

Best wishes from all of us here in the Neighborhood.

Sincerely,

Fred Rogers

MISTER ROGERS' NEIGHBORHOOD is underwritten by Public Television Stations
and the Corporation for Public Broadcasting.

Fred Rogers
Television Personality (Mister Rogers)

Burgess Meredith

November 10, 1995

I HAVE NO DEFINITION OF SUCCESS - EVERYONE IS ON HIS OWN!
GOOD LUCK!

Burgess Meredith
Actor

Conrad Bain

SUCCESS

Success is whatever you think it is, or perhaps what you want it to be. A person born with defects, physical or mental, may feel that he or she is successful in achieving the most modest goals of survival and a modicum of acceptance. Whereas a person with a masters degree in business that is stuck in middle management and making a very good living, may feel like a failure. Success is in the soul of the successful.

Because we live in a marketplace society, we are taught to compete successfully and strive for excellence, therefore to be a success. Unfortunately, we are not taught how to adjust our lives and our view of ourselves if those objectives are not met. This results in countless people ending up feeling like failures, since only the few are destined to win. I would suggest that children, should be encouraged, early in life, to begin to formulate their own ideas of what success means to them.

Speaking for myself, it was my belief that if I could be privileged to do the work I love, earn some kind of living at it, and find love in marriage and perhaps a family, then I would feel that I was successful. Great notoriety, the accumulation of wealth, an extravagant life style, and other apparently conventional symbols of success, were never included in my personal image of success. Looking back among my friends and acquaintances it is evident that these things seldom bring contentment.

Too often I think influences outside of self create one's image of success. Parents, with the best intentions of course, may influence a young person in their idea of success which may be inappropriate, because the parent may be expressing unfulfilled ambitions of their own. A concept of success is better arrived at without the element of fear. Fear that you won't measure up, that you won't be rich, that you won't be noticed, or respected, or admired or loved. A concept of success that germinates from fear can never deliver genuine contentment.

Successful living, is only a reflection of the fulfillment of the inner person. That surely is success.

Sincerely,

Conrad Bain

Conrad Bain
Actor

THE GOVERNOR OF THE STATE OF FLORIDA

December 14, 1995

LAWTON CHILES

Throughout my life I've served the people of my state. That privilege has taken me on a personally, spiritually rewarding journey -- first to the Florida Legislature, then to the United States Senate and finally back home to the governor's mansion. My life's work has been all about helping people succeed. I've always tried to give back more than I have received. For me, the definition of success lies in the faces of the people I have worked to help and in the beauty of the communities I have worked to strengthen.

When I walked from the Florida Panhandle to the Keys during the 1970 U.S. Senate campaign, I wanted to meet the people and hear their concerns. That walk made me a better senator -- and it has made me a better governor, too.

One of my proudest achievements is my work to strengthen Florida's families. During my walk, I heard the people say they wanted their children to have a better world. As senator, I worked to create the National Commission to Prevent Infant Mortality. As governor, I took what I learned as the chair of the commission to start Florida's landmark Healthy Start program.

Today, Healthy Start offers prenatal and health care to every pregnant woman and infant child in Florida. This effort is helping us build a healthy generation in Florida -- and has played an important role in lowering our infant mortality rate to its lowest point in history. Nearly 800 children have escaped becoming a tragic statistic because of our efforts to reduce infant mortality in Florida. That's the equivalent of 35 kindergarten classrooms. I am proud of that fact and I am committed to redouble our efforts to reduce infant mortality rate in Florida.

Healthy Start is a strong example of what success for our children is all about. We are committed to improving the lives of our children -- by investing in their future. I believe we can help ourselves by helping others. That's why I'm committed to policies that enrich the lives of all our people. I believe it's that same dedication to sharing achievement with the community that will help all of us as our nation faces the challenges of the next century.

With kind regards, I am

Sincerely,

Lawton Chiles

LAWTON CHILES

Lawton Chiles
Governor of Florida

PAUL D. COVERDELL
GEORGIA

United States Senate
WASHINGTON, DC 20510–1004

November 29, 1995

Thank you for the opportunity to participate in your "giving back the dream" project.

Success means many things to many people. Some think that it is measured only in monetary standards, while others think that is based on career achievements. Whatever it may be, success can not be achieved unless one is committed to following the criteria for success. I use the word criteria because I believe that there are four basic fundamentals leading to success: pay attention to detail, be persistent, do your homework, and most importantly, work hard. Following these basic fundamentals is itself a sign of success and will take you wherever you want to go.

Personally, success was achieved the day I became financially able to care for my parents, should the need arise.

Again, thank you for your interest and best wishes for every continued success.

Sincerely,

Paul D. Coverdell
United States Senator

Paul D. Coverdell
U.S. Senator from Georgia

David Carradine Entertainment

November 29, 1995

My Definition of Success

To set a goal and then surpass it.
Know what you want.
Learn what you need to know.
Build your mind, your body, your spirit.
Go for it with all your heart.
Take chances.
Be ready always to change.
Follow through.
Patience, strength, fortitude.
Don't give up.

Peace

David Carradine

David Carradine

David Carradine
Actor

OFFICE OF THE GOVERNOR
STATE CAPITOL
SANTA FE, NEW MEXICO 87503

GARY E. JOHNSON
GOVERNOR

(505) 827-3000

NEW MEXICO GOVERNOR GARY E. JOHNSON' S DEFINITON OF SUCCESS

Success is a word that does not have a universal definition. I feel that success is directly linked to happiness. Real success lies in the ability to state that you are truly happy. There are several aspects in my life that truly make me happy. The fact that I have the family that I have, especially my wife and my two children, is a large part of the reason that I am happy. Another aspect of happiness is the fact that I am financially able to provide for my family by keeping a roof over our heads, food on our table and gas in our car. Being in good physical condition is another part of my life that truly makes me happy. In addition, there are three basic provisions that I have always maintained in both my personal and professional life. They are as follows: telling the truth, keeping my word and remaining accountable for my actions. Always holding true to these three things allows me to be happy with myself. This combination makes it possible for me to achieve success.

Gary E. Johnson
Governor of New Mexico

In summation, there is only one person responsible for making you happy, and that is you. It is my thinking that if one reiterates and incorporates daily the things in life that truly make one happy, then one has attained true success.

Thank you for your time. I wish you happiness in all of your future endeavors.

Sincerely,

Gary E. Johnson
Governor of New Mexico

Gary E. Johnson
Governor of New Mexico

Laura Huxley
Founder / President

Dr. Piero Ferrucci
Director

TO LOVE AND TO BE LOVED

What is success? Success is: *to love and to be loved.*

In 1960 I wrote:

*"The essentials for **bare** living are food, water, and air. What is the essential for **happy** living? We hear the answer continuously:*

> *I want to be loved.*
> *I want to love.*
> *I want to be loved.*
> *I want to love.*

Disguised in a thousand forms, hidden under an infinite variety of masks, love starvation is even more rampant than food starvation. It invades all classes and all peoples. It occurs in all climates, on every social and economic level. It seems to occur in all forms of life. Love starvation wears the stony face of the disciplinarian or speaks in the hysterical voice of the zealot. It puts on the unctuous manner of the hypocrite or the ruthlessness of the ambitious power seeker.

*Love starvation may camouflage itself in physical and mental ills, in delinquency, sometimes in death. In a family, love starvation begets love starvation in one generation after another until a rebel in that family breaks the malevolent chain. If you find yourself in such a family, BE THAT REBEL." ***

After thirty-five years of intense living and loving, which includes suffering anxiety, sickness and death, I can only confirm that successful living is:*to love and to be loved - -* and that, if we find, whether in family or nation, a 'NOT LOVE' situation, then peacefully courageously unshakably we REBEL and remain In Love.

Laura Huxley

* *Your Are Not The Target* -- Farrar, Straus & Company 1963
Metamorphous Press P.O. Box 10616 Portland, Oregon 97210-0616 -- paperback

O U R   U L T I M A T E   I N V E S T M E N T
A non-profit organization for the nurturing of the possible human

Laura Huxley
Founder and President, Our Ultimate Investment

PRISON
FELLOWSHIP.
Ministries

November 21, 1995

I achieved success by the world's standards. I earned a scholarship through Brown University, graduated with honors; earned a Juris Doctor degree at night, again with honors; was a company commander in the Marines; the youngest administrative assistant in the United States Senate; senior partner in a large and thriving law firm; and at age 39, an assistant to the President, sitting in the office immediately next to his. I was the grandson of an immigrant and my life was the American dream fulfilled.

It was only when I achieved all of those things that I realized how empty they really were. I was seeking to find meaning in life through power, influence, money, stature and politics, and I failed. I had success, but I also had a tremendous hole inside of me. I discovered that it was a spiritual vacuum. In prison with all the things of this world stripped away, I found the only security and meaning and purpose a person ever knows--a personal relationship with the living God, Jesus Christ.

On looking back, I can honestly say that I never met anyone the entire time I was in government who told me that their life had been affected by anything I had done--at least for the good. By contrast, I've met hundreds, maybe thousands, since I've been in Christian service, whose lives God has chosen to touch through my life and virtually through my biggest defeat, going to prison.

How would I today define success? Certainly not the way I did in the first forty years of my life. Now success to me is believing, following and serving God, and being at peace with Him. I keep a plaque on my desk that reminds me of what I believe to be the principal calling of the Christian. It reads "Faithfulness Not Success."

Yours in His service,

Charles W. Colson

"A bruised reed he will not break . . .
In faithfulness he will bring forth justice."
Isaiah 42:3

Charles W. Colson
Religious Leader/Counsel to President Nixon

December 1st, 1995

DAVID BENOIT

Re: my definition of success.

When I was about 14 years old, I wanted to be a famous jazz pianist more than anything. I remember seeing a movie called "The Nutty Professor" where Jerry Lewis went from being a shy geeky school teacher to an elegant, debonair character who could dazzle people by playing the piano. I thought that was the coolest thing to be. I also loved movie soundtracks, so I set a goal for myself that by the time I reached 40, I would score a major motion picture. (I accomplished that goal when I was 41, but who's counting.)

Anyway, I think success is probably doing what you really want to do albeit all the and ups and downs along the way. When I think of success I think of opportunity, preparation, talent and luck.

Sincerely,

David Benoit

David Benoit
Composer

Phyllis Diller

SUCCESS means different things to various people. For some it is wealth, for some power, for others a blooming garden, travel, freedom to be solo and be completely responsible only to yourself, or friends or maybe all of these elements.

However, real success is happiness. You enjoy what you have and are satisfied, fulfilled and peaceful.

— *Phyllis Diller*
1995

Phyllis Diller
Comedienne/Actress

STATE OF MISSISSIPPI
OFFICE OF THE GOVERNOR

KIRK FORDICE
GOVERNOR

November 7, 1995

Thank you for this outstanding opportunity to share with fellow Americans my idea of success. Rudyard Kipling is one of my favorite authors, and his poem, "IF" is one of my favorite poems. In fact, I have often quoted this poem in speeches to the citizens of Mississippi. I believe that all young people benefit from exposure to this unique articulation of the genuine spirit of success. Although times have changed dramatically since Kipling's era and we must understand the closing line of his poem as *universally* applicable--not directed strictly to the male gender, but to *all* human beings--this poem articulates ideas and values that work to the benefit of all who partake of its beauty.

Sincerely,

KIRK FORDICE
Governor

POST OFFICE BOX 139 • JACKSON, MISSISSIPPI 39205 • TEL: (601) 359-3150 • FAX (601) 359-3741

Kirk Fordice
Governor of Mississippi

If

RUDYARD KIPLING

(Born December 30, 1865; died January 17, 1936)

If you can keep your head when all about you
   Are losing theirs and blaming it on you;
If you can trust yourself when all men doubt you,
   But make allowance for their doubting too:
If you can wait and not be tired by waiting,
   Or, being lied about, don't deal in lies.
Or being hated don't give way to hating,
   And yet don't look too good, nor talk too wise;

If you can dream—and not make dreams your master:
   If you can think—and not make thoughts your aim,
If you can meet with Triumph and Disaster
   And treat those two impostors just the same:
If you can bear to hear the truth you've spoken
   Twisted by knaves to make a trap for fools,
Or watch the things you gave your life to, broken,
   And stoop and build 'em up with worn-out tools;

If you can make one heap of all your winnings
   And risk it on one turn of pitch-and-toss.
And lose, and start again at your beginnings,
   And never breathe a word about your loss:
If you can force your heart and nerve and sinew
   To serve your turn long after they are gone,
And so hold on when there is nothing in you
   Except the Will which says to them: "Hold on!"

If you can talk with crowds and keep your virtue,
   Or walk with Kings—nor lose the common touch,
If neither foes nor loving friends can hurt you,
   If all men count with you, but none too much:
If you can fill the unforgiving minute
   With sixty seconds' worth of distance run,
Yours is the Earth and everything that's in it,
   And—which is more—you'll be a Man, my son!

Kirk Fordice

Governor of Mississippi

Success

A dream which comes alive
Is a passing breath
And a longed for wish
Wish true and wish forgotten
Life is the constant beat
of the heart of one
That reveals your road
your road to follow
Your one true path
yours alone
Unique to one
And shared by all
It is our grand success

Mariel Hemingway

Mariel Hemingway
Actress

BLADES PRODUCTIONS

October 31, 1995

Rather than advance into the philosophical quicksand of defining
what success is, perhaps it is more prudent to present a descrip-
tion of failure. I believe to fail is not to try.
Success is but a perception, impossible to categorize with any degree of lasting certainty. Therefore, what others consider succes-
ful should not necessarily influence our interpretation of life, or
world events.
Some of the most humiliating defeats can ultimately become the source
of inspiration out of which the most absolute victories draw from
(Dunkirk is a clear example).
On the other end, some public triumphs, like that of Mr. O.J. Simpson's
legal team, have been received with as much bitterness as elation.
The term success implies that there are winners and losers. And yet
there are no absolute affirmations of continuity for either one of
these extremes: what we celebrate today may return tomorrow to des-
troy us, what we yesterday considered a defeat may become a needed
step towards personal fulfillment.

In 1994 I ran for president in my native country, Panamá, and came in
third in a field of seven candidates, (our new party, Papa Egoró, came
in third out of seventeen political parties).
Although we lost the election, we won national and international respect
by forever dismantling the myth of the invincibility of traditional
party structures and tactics which have monopolized political discourse
in Latin America. By not succumbing to their corruption, we freed ourselves from the alleged inevitability of their existence.
I do not know what success is. I do know what failure is: failure is not
to try. That's my definition of "success".

Sincerely,

R. Blades

Rubén Blades

Rubén Blades
Conductor/Actor

15 NOVEMBER 1995

The definition of success is as difficult to define as it is to attain. It can be as tiny as a baby taking its first step, or as magnificent as finding a cure for polio. There is success in the miraculous moment a child is born, or there is the awe of having received 20 gold records. Success is being realistic with yourself, but never giving up on your dreams. It's learning how to love and be loved. Often success comes from hard work, or luck, and sometimes success is as illusive and colorful as a rainbow. But one thing is most certain--if you are truly successful you will know it, because you can feel it in your heart.

Andy Williams
Singer/Songwriter

from the desk of
<u>Kirk Cameron</u>

December 3, 1995

Thank you for opportunity to be a part of this wonderful project to further "give back the dream." I hope you find this helpful and appropriate for your book.

Success is accomplishing what it is you set out to do. Personally, I never set out to be the best actor in the world, nor did I set out to be rich or famous. For me, I am setting out to have integrity. My life is the opportunity to accomplish this and one day I'll ask God if I was successful.

Sincerely,

Kirk Cameron

Kirk Cameron
Actor

COMMONWEALTH OF KENTUCKY
OFFICE OF THE GOVERNOR

BRERETON C. JONES
GOVERNOR

THE CAPITOL
700 CAPITAL AVENUE
FRANKFORT 40601
(502) 564-2611

November 9, 1995

Thank you for your letter and invitation to participate in the project featuring "success" stories. I am delighted to offer the following thoughts:

Success is achieving a favorable result from a particular effort. Too often we are short-sighted or self-centered with our efforts and even though we achieve our goals, we are not satisfied with what we thought was our success.

Let me give an example. If our goal is to be rich and we achieve our goal, we are dissatisfied if we discover that we are not happy.

Therefore, true success is not just in achieving a certain goal. True success comes when we achieve worthwhile goals that bring comfort and happiness to others. If our goal is to be rich for selfish reasons and we are successful, we will have failed. If our goal is to be rich for humanitarian reasons and we are successful, we will have succeeded.

With best regards, I am

Sincerely,

Brereton C. Jones

AN EQUAL OPPORTUNITY EMPLOYER M/F/D

Brereton C. Jones
Governor of Kentucky

Formula for Success

I once read a book about several people who made it to the very top of their professions. In analyzing their success, I found it surprising to realize there was a common formula that ran through each of their lives.

1. Each one loved the work and felt that the very worst thing that could happen was not being able to go to work the next day.

2. Each one thrived on the work and didn't really consider it work at all—but pleasure!

3. Each one had failed at one time or another and was able to accept failure, considering it just another opportunity to try again.

4. All were highly competitive and wanted to be at the top of their professions. None of them liked to lose.

5. All were extroverts or had become that way in the process of pursuing their goals.

6. Each one had good work habits, knew how to make the most of time and how to follow through.

7. All knew what they wanted and would let nothing stop them.

To this list I would add faith or belief. No matter what problems you have, you can overcome them. I truly believe that if you show me someone who has made it big, I can show you someone who probably shouldn't have made it at all.

Success is a constantly varying idea held in the mind of each individual. Our personal goals regulate the success we plan to achieve. If we set our goals for the highest possible achievements and follow a few basic steps, we are each destined for success.

My Wage

I bargained with Life for a penny,
And Life would pay no more,
However I begged at evening
When I counted my scanty store;

For Life is a just employer,
He gives you what you ask,
But once you have set the wages,
Why, you must bear the task.

I worked for a menial's hire,
Only to learn, dismayed,
That any wage I had asked of Life,
Life would have paid.

—*Jessie B. Rittenhouse*

Mary Kay Ash
Founder, Mary Kay Cosmetics

Albert Reynolds, T.D.

sh, November 1995
AR/MC

My recipe for success:

Find a market, fill it as opportunity comes to pass and do not
pause.

Best wishes,

ALBERT REYNOLDS, T.D.

Albert Reynolds
Prime Minister of Ireland

17 June 1996

Sucess is defined not by the standard, but by the individual.

It is the continous fulfillment of one's potential; liking yourself; loving your family; enjoying what you do; giving to others and having balance in your life.

If you can achieve the above you are truly a successful person.

Rocky Bleier

Rocky Bleier
Professional Football Player/Businessman

Carlson Companies Inc.

Curtis L. Carlson
Chairman & Chief Executive Officer

June 14, 1996

My Definition of Success:

If you can find the type of work you love to do, from that day on, you will never "work" another day in your life.

In my own case, when I went into business for myself with Gold Bond and Top Value trading stamps, I found myself anxious to get to work, leaving reluctantly to go home, and I had the following personal business philosophy:

"Working the first five days of the week you stay even with your competition, but the sixth day is when you get ahead."

Curt Carlson

Curtis L. Carlson
Founder, Chairman and CEO, Carlson Companies

ERNEST borgNiNE

TREAT YOUR FELLOW MAN AS YOU

WOULD TREAT YOURSELF, BECAUSE

A SMILE AND A KIND WORD MAKES

A WORLD OF DIFFERENCE.

November, 1995

Ernest Borgnine
Actor

ERNEST F. HOLLINGS
SOUTH CAROLINA

OFFICES:

1835 ASSEMBLY STREET
COLUMBIA, SC 29201
803-765-5731

103 FEDERAL BUILDING
SPARTANBURG, SC 29301
803-585-3702

126 FEDERAL BUILDING
GREENVILLE, SC 29603
803-233-5366

112 CUSTOM HOUSE
200 EAST BAY STREET
CHARLESTON, SC 29401
803-727-4525

United States Senate

125 RUSSELL OFFICE BUILDING
WASHINGTON, DC 20510-4002
202-224-6121

July 1, 1996

COMMITTEES:

COMMERCE, SCIENCE, AND
TRANSPORTATION: RANKING

APPROPRIATIONS
COMMERCE, JUSTICE, STATE AND
THE JUDICIARY: RANKING
DEFENSE
LABOR, HEALTH AND HUMAN SERVICES,
EDUCATION
ENERGY AND WATER DEVELOPMENT
INTERIOR

BUDGET

DEMOCRATIC POLICY COMMITTEE

OFFICE OF TECHNOLOGY ASSESSMENT

NATIONAL OCEAN POLICY STUDY

Dear Friends:

Having dedicated the better part of my life to public service, I would define success as an ongoing process. People's achievements in life should not measured in terms of how much money or power they have, but in terms of what they are able to do with it. If I am to be considered a success, it is not because I am a U.S. senator, but because as a senator, I have had the chance to fight for the rights and freedoms of people in my own state and all over the country.

There is a quotation by Robert Lewis Stevenson which I think sums it up nicely, "To travel hopefully is a better thing than to arrive, and the true success is to labor."

With kindest regards, I am

Sincerely,

Fritz Hollings

Ernest F. Hollings

PRINTED ON RECYCLED PAPER

Ernest F. Hollings
U.S. Senator from South Carolina

D. James Kennedy
A.B., M.Div., M.Th., D.D., D.Sac.Lit., Ph.D.,
Litt.D., D.Sac.Theol., D. Humane Let.

June 27, 1996

Senior Minister
Coral Ridge Presbyterian Church

Chancellor
Knox Theological Seminary

President
Evangelism Explosion
International

President & Speaker
Coral Ridge Ministries
Television and Radio

Thank you for the invitation to have my definition
of success included in the inspirational collection
your organization is planning to publish. My definition
follows:

> Success in my mind is having used the
> intelligence and gifts that God has
> given to you to the best of your ability
> to accomplish God's purposes in this
> world to the glory of His name.

Thank you for writing to me.

Sincerely in Christ,

D. James Kennedy, Ph.D.
Senior Minister

D. James Kennedy
Religious Leader

State of North Dakota

OFFICE OF THE GOVERNOR
600 E. BOULEVARD — GROUND FLOOR
BISMARCK, NORTH DAKOTA 58505-0001
(701) 328-2200
FAX (701) 328-2205   TDD (701) 328-2887

EDWARD T. SCHAFER
GOVERNOR

June 26, 1996

There is only one definition for success. My father, Harold Schafer, always had a little wooden box on his desk. On it, it said "The Secret of Success." Inside, one word was printed: work!

I must have looked at that box a thousand times when I was growing up, and today I cannot think of a more true statement. The secret to success is work.

Thank you for the opportunity to participate in this project, and best wishes to your organization and Make-A-Wish Foundation.

Sincerely,

Edward T. Schafer
Governor

Edward T. Schafer
Governor of North Dakota

ROBERT MONDAVI WINERY   OAKVILLE, CALIFORNIA

June 21, 1996

I appreciate the opportunity to discuss my definition of success for The Make-A-Wish Foundation.

Success is not, in my mind, to be evaluated with achievement, but rather in a commitment to excel. Achievements will come along the way.

In my personal experience, the seeds of success were planted by my parents, who taught me to try my best and be tenacious in my attempts; this meant a commitment to excel. The defining issue was the goal of proving to the world that we could make wines that ranked with the best in the world here in Napa Valley. I knew we had the soil, the climate and the grape varieties that could produce those wines; what was needed was greater winemaking knowledge and experience, and the strong desire to excel.

Happily we have accomplished those things, and to the point that others come to us for knowledge and experience now.

I wish much success to the Institute for Successful Living in its work.

Sincerely,

Robert Mondavi

NAPA VALLEY WINES

Robert Mondavi
Founder, Robert Mondavi Winery

CHET ATKINS

I have had success beyond any degree I ever imagined. It probably happened because of a lot of good luck and the fact that I loved guitar, never thought of monetary enrichment, practiced constantly, and for several years, I didn't know what other players were doing. So a style developed that has served me so very well. There is nothing but gratefulness to all those folks, who for fifty years have supported my habit of PLAYING GUITAR.

Chet Atkins, c.g.p.

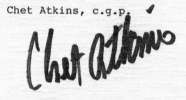

Chet Atkins
Guitarist/Singer

STATE OF MARYLAND
OFFICE OF THE GOVERNOR

PARRIS N. GLENDENING
GOVERNOR

ANNAPOLIS OFFICE
STATE HOUSE
100 STATE CIRCLE
ANNAPOLIS, MARYLAND 21401
(410) 974-3901

WASHINGTON OFFICE
SUITE 311
444 NORTH CAPITOL STREET, N.W.
WASHINGTON, D.C. 20001
(202) 638-2215

TDD (410) 333-3098

July 1, 1996

Thank you for your recent letter about your research and information you are gathering to define success. I am honored to be among the distinguished participants in your study. I certainly agree that we can all learn so much from one another.

It is my belief that our future is found in a single word--education. In Gaithersburg, Maryland, there is a small plaque on a wall inside the Washington Grove Elementary School which reads: "A school is a building with four walls and tomorrow inside." I would not be where I am today had it not been for education. My dad did not go to college. He worked two jobs, sometimes three, to keep a family of six children together. He always stressed I would be successful if I did well in my education and went to college. He shared a fundamental part of the American dream - that our children will do better, they will be better off because of education. My dad died when I was still an undergraduate at Florida State University. He never had a chance to see the dream come true. I am here today because my dad was right. All those parents who dream of a better future through education for their children are also right.

Sincerely,

Parris N. Glendening

Parris N. Glendening
Governor

Parris N. Glendening
Governor of Maryland

Solomon Tandeng Muna
Retired President of the National Assembly of the Republic of Cameroon
Former PrimeMinister of West Cameroon
Former Vice-President of the Federal Republic of Cameroon
Former Co-President of theACP-EEC Consultative Assembly
Fellow of the Baden-Powell Scout Foundation

I was born during the period of German colonization of my country, Cameroon, to parents who had known no other world but theirs, who had known no other culture but theirs and who had known no other gods but theirs. After the Germans lost the great war, the British took over Cameroon and shortly thereafter I went to school, loosing both my parents within the first years of primary school. Now I was being revealed a new world, a new culture and a new God. I was introduced to Christian religion and was struck very early on by Matt. 6.33 "But seek ye first the Kingdom of God and His righteousness and all these things shall be added unto you."

I have spent my whole professional life as a teacher and as a politician. These two professions have provided me with much happiness and satisfaction in life, because in these two professions people were my prime concern and preoccupation. As a teacher I tried to shape young minds so that they may grow up to be successful and useful citizens within the society. As a politician I tried to build a just and fair society in

Solomon Tandeng Muna
Prime Minister of West Cameroon

which citizens could live in harmony and in happiness.   In both cases, it is not what I did but how I did it that mattered.   My actions and way of life had to be reflected by my beliefs, my teaching, and my philosophy of life.   To have had a partner who shared my beliefs made it easier.

My real success did not lie in the fact that I became a successful teacher or politician, although this was the evidence of it, on the physical plane, real success lay in the fact of my accepting to undertake a journey into the unknown.   In accepting to discover a new world, a new culture, and a new religion.   Real success does not come from fathoming and solidyfing the known.   It comes from making life an adventure of discovery, with humankind as the central objective, with faith in God as the compass.   On this journey you will recognize the milestones   of   love,   generosity,   honesty,   kindness, respectfulness,   humility, sympathy, cleanliness, patience, laughter, tears, hardwork and respect.   It is a journey not without hurdles and pitfalls, false trails and distractions which may deceive you in believing you have arrived.   Because it is a journey into infinity, into the unfathomable essence of life and the immeasurable Kingdom of God, you acquire many things on this long journey, including riches, happiness, satisfaction, honour, praise, recognition and, above all, peace and unity with humankind.   I am 84 years old and I am still journeying on, even though I have a prosperous family

2

Solomon Tandeng Muna
Prime Minister of West Cameroon

where happiness and unity reigns and we share our prosperity and enjoy rendering service to our fellow man.   I am still going for infinity towards the source of life and trying to fulfill the purpose of my being on this planet.

Success is reaching your potential, no matter how small you think the part is, you will be amazed the amount of light and happiness it can bring into other people's lives.   True success comes from believing in yourself, and that your life on earth has a purpose, and other human beings are the object of that purpose. The abandonment self and faith in God is a good start in life's adventure.

When success comes, it overwhelms you with wonder and satisfaction and you are amazed that that was your doing.   It gives you complete satisfaction because success knows no half measures, for it is like pregnancy, you cannot be a little bit pregnant.

As I continue life's adventure into infinity, into the unfathomable essence of God's Kingdom, I am amazed at all that has been added unto me, at the richness of life that surrounds me, at the honour and recognition that friends accord me.   I am amazed that still running the race of life, I have been declared a winner. This is not a time to stop and receive the laurels, with all humility I stumble on. Real success is being declared a winner when we are still in the course of the race of life.

3

Solomon Tandeng Muna
Prime Minister of West Cameroon

I will end with a quote, from *Ralph Waldo Emerson*:

"To laugh often and love much; to win the respect of intelligent persons and the affection of children; to earn the appreciation of honest critics; to endure the betrayal of false friends; to appreciate beauty; to find the best in others; leave this world a little bit better whether by a healthy child, a garden patch, or a redeemed social condition; to know even one has breathed easier because you have lived-this is success."

SOLOMON TANDENG MUNA
Mbengwi June 16, 1996

Solomon Tandeng Muna
Prime Minister of West Cameroon

Bell Labs
Innovations for Lucent Technologies

Lucent Technologies

Arno Penzias
Vice President
Chief Scientist

How can you tell how successful you are? Take a mental poll of the people whose opinions you value. What do they think of you and what you have accomplished (or would think of you if they knew of you)?

You get to pick the list. Include yourself, I think, because a person without a sense of self seems hollow inside. The choices you make—teachers, family members, neighbors, colleagues, role models— says much about yourself and what success means to you.

Arno Penzias

Arno Penzias
Nobel Prize in Physics Laureate

MICHAEL YORK

" Success is the outward
manifestation of
inward fulfillment "

Michael York
Actor

STICHTING
INTERNATIONAL FINANCIAL SERVICES

DR. J. SEDNEY 475010   Bankers: ABN-AMRO

Paramaribo, June 27, 1996.

I am very honoured to have been selected for a contribution to your project.

Here is my definition of success.

> "Success is the ultimate reward for hard work,
> honest behaviour and clean living.
> Success does not come by acccident or incident,
> but only through concentration and dedication".

Sincerely Yours,

Dr. J. Sedney,

Address:
Maystraat 34
Paramaribo-Suriname
Tel./fax 597-421029

Jules Sedney
Prime Minister of Suriname

BARBARA A. MIKULSKI
MARYLAND

COMMITTEES:

APPROPRIATIONS

LABOR AND HUMAN RESOURCES

SUITE 709
HART SENATE OFFICE BUILDING
WASHINGTON, DC 20510-2003
(202) 224-4654
TTY: (202) 224-5223

United States Senate
WASHINGTON, DC 20510-2003

STATEMENT BY SENATOR BARBARA MIKULSKI

"Defining Success"

It is easy to measure success by the balance in one's bank account or the square footage in one's house. But often the real measure of success comes through accomplishments and achievements that cannot be quantified so easily.

My father taught me that true success requires a day-by-day measurement: Each night, as my family sat around the dinner table, he would ask me if I had learned something that day. I should gauge my success, he said, by my answer. Over the years, I have added another question: "Did I make someone's life better today?" If I can say "yes" to that question, I feel I have been successful.

As a United States Senator, I measure my greatest successes by saving lives and saving communities in Maryland. Whether it was saving historic Baltimore neighborhoods, including the first African-American home-ownership community, from being torn down to make way for a 16-lane highway or saving a local World War II hero's veteran's benefits, I know I have worked hard to make someone's life better. That is the most rewarding form of success and I thank my father for the inspiration.

Barbara A. Mikulski
United States Senator

WORLD TRADE CENTER, SUITE 253
401 E. PRATT STREET
BALTIMORE, MD 21202-3099
(410) 962-4510

60 WEST STREET, SUITE 202
ANNAPOLIS, MD 21401-2448
(410) 263-1805

9658 BALTIMORE AVENUE, SUITE 207
COLLEGE PARK, MD 20740-1346
(301) 345-5517

62 WEST WASHINGTON STREET, SUITE 301
HAGERSTOWN, MD 21740-4804
(301) 797-2826

SUITE 1E, BUILDING B
1201 PEMBERTON DRIVE
SALISBURY, MD 21801-2403
(410) 546-7711

PRINTED ON RECYCLED PAPER

Barbara A. Mikulski
U.S. Senator from Maryland

First African Methodist Episcopal Church

"FIRST TO SERVE"

Dr. Cecil L. Murray MINISTER

July 9, 1996

A DEFINITION OF SUCCESS

We called him "Single Wing," a name he adored and adorned more than his natural identification. He was missing his left arm, yet played first base for the freshman team at Florida A & M University, 1947. He would catch the ball with his gloved right hand, cradle the mitt under the opposite armpit, snatch the ball from the ensnared mitt with his all-purpose right hand, then throw across the field for a double play at second base or third base. Nobody stole home—or anything else—on Single Wing, nobody.

He was the bumblebee who didn't realize he was an aerodynamic impossibility. So he just flew. He was "Wheel," doing artful pirouettes in his wheelchair, redefining the word invalid, and defining the word success: success is taking the thing working against you and forcing it to work for you.

Success is hearing the angels shout as you cross the finish line with style --

> Go, Wheel . . .
> > Go, Bumblebee . . .
> > > Go, Single Wing . . .
> > > > Go!

Sincerely,

Cecil L. "Chip" Murray
Cecil L. "Chip" Murray
Senior Minister

"GOD OUR FATHER, CHRIST OUR REDEEMER, MAN OUR BROTHER"

Cecil L. Murray
Religious Leader

July 1, 1996

Good Friends:

Thank you so much for your recent letter to Bob Keeshan (Captain Kangaroo). He was pleased to learn that you would like to include his thoughts on success in your forthcoming publication.

The words I am quoting below are Mr. Keeshan's own, and he has asked me to send them along to you with the hope that they will be of some small use to you:

"Appreciate your uniqueness. Never in history has there been anyone exactly like you. Being one of a kind you must be the best you possibly can be; develop your talents to the fullest. You can do anything you wish to do; the only limitation is your will. Make the most of the one and only you."

Mr. Keeshan thanks you again for thinking of him, and sends his warmest and sincerest good wishes.

Cordially,

Laura Ramsey
for
Bob Keeshan

Bob Keeshan
Television Personality (Captain Kangaroo)

United Way
of America

Elaine L. Chao
President and Chief Executive Officer

June 28, 1996

My definition of success is molded to a great degree by the example of my parents, Dr. and Mrs. James S. C. Chao. They are people of great integrity, faith, and courage. As a young couple in their 20s, they left everything familiar -- their family, friends, culture, country, language, and even diet -- to seek a new life of opportunity in America. Faced with many challenges, they never forsook the belief that America was a land of generosity and decency. With hard work, they knew they would make a better future for themselves and their children. We, their children, grew up imbued with this sense of optimism, confidence and determination. My parents also instilled within us a sense of responsibility and service to our community.

I am fortunate to have had the guidance and counsel of these two great individuals. To me, success in life means being a credit to my loved ones, my community and my people. Success in life also means service and contribution to my community.

Sincerely,

Elaine L. Chao

United Way of America Mission: To support and serve local United Ways to help increase the
organized capacity of people to care for one another.

Elaine L. Chao
President and CEO, United Way of America

To feel true success
Find an inner
Joy of Self.

Life is full of
material illusions
which cannot
buy success.

True Success
comes
from within.

Tova Borgnine
CEO, Tova Corporation

July 15, 1996

The Roar Foundation
Shambala Preserve

I would like to provide you with a quote or personal experience - I'm not quite sure which this would be:

I have found that during my lifetime, it has become more and more apparent to me that one need not make a choice in life to do a specific thing for a lifetime. The fact that you can be flexible and move from one career to another has been an incredibly important part of my life and makes for a natural flow of growing.

I went from being a fashion model to an actress, which culminated in what I feel is my true life's work, which is being involved with saving many, many incredibly beautiful animals from having a miserable life, by being director of the Shambala Preserve and president of the Roar Foundation, which funds the Shambala Preserve.

Living with these magnificent animals has given me probably the most important extension of my life.

Basically what I feel that I am saying is, allow yourself a free mind and don't be afraid, so that you can experience new things in your life. Change is GOOD! It's a growth-building experience and one that can be extremely effective and it can also keep you very young.

Warmly,

Tippi Hedren

Tippi Hedren
Actress

Kenny Bernstein's
Budweiser King Racing

My Definition of Success

By Kenny Bernstein

Auto racing is a team sport in its purest sense. It's impossible to win an individual race, let alone a championship, without many people all working productively toward a common goal.

I've found that the same ingredients necessary to win on the racetrack also apply to achieving success in other aspects of life.

Among these elements is working as hard as is required in order to achieve the desired goal. This also implies a willingness to go the extra mile in delivering more value, service or results than expected -- a guaranteed way to set yourself apart from the rest.

To the greatest degree possible, attempt to control your own destiny through attention to detail and a willingness to take responsibility for the outcome of each task.

Keep your mind open to new ideas and different opinions, and take the time to weigh pros and cons before reaching a decision. Become an effective communicator and encourage those skills among those you work with.

Don't allow yourself to be swept away by the highs of your victories or the lows of your defeats. Instead, analyze each and try to learn something that will help you in the future.

Success rarely happens accidentally. The above tools have been indispensable to me both on and off the racetrack.

Sincerely,

Kenny Bernstein

Kenny Bernstein
Race-Car Driver

ENTERPRISES, L.L.C.

November 13, 1995

I will be happy to give you a quote concerning our success story.

   "Success to me is defined in three ways. 1.) People, 2). People, 3.) People. In today's world of short-term planning and the gready quest for the fast dollar, we lose sight of what it takes to build a successful institution. No doubt, it takes strategic planning, bright people, but just as importantly, a sensitivity to the organization and its goals that allows everyone to participate. To get commitment from an organization, regardless of the size of the institution, requires leadership that believes in people, people, people."

J. E. Antonini

J. E. Antonini
President and CEO, K-Mart Corporation

PEALE CENTER
FOR CHRISTIAN LIVING

Dedicated to the Advancement of Christianity as a Practical Way of Life

RUTH STAFFORD PEALE
Chairman of the Board

August 21, 1996

Success is the fulfillment of a person's
potential. Keeping on doing what one does
best tends to magnify achievement and often
brings astonishing results.

Ruth Stafford Peale

Ruth Stafford Peale
Chairman of the Board, Peale Center for Christian Living

ARTIE SHAW

"Success (as opposed to $ucce$$) is making your living at what you would do even if you weren't paid to do it."

Artie Shaw

Artie Shaw
Jazz Clarinetist

MICHAEL DAVID WARD
P R O D U C T I O N S ,   I N C

July 24, 1996

The following is a distillation of the true essence for what I believe to be the secret to success and a happy life:

"Follow the truth in your heart, whatever that may be, so long as it stirs passion in your life and fuels the inner drive that is in each of our souls. Follow that and no matter where you are our what your doing, you'll be happy in the pursuit."

Sincerely,

Michael David Ward
Artist/President

Michael David Ward
Artist

UNIVERSITY OF ZIMBABWE

July 19 1996

For me, success is based on selfless love and service to humanity. The short poem below for me has been an important characteristic of success.

> Love all and hate none,
> Be friend to all and enemy to none.
> Respect all and despise none,
> Understand all and misunderstand none.
> Support all and neglect none.

With all good wishes

Yours sincerely

C. S. Banana

Canaan Sodindo Banana
First President of Zimbabwe
Eminent Person-Organisation of African Unity.

Canaan Sodindo Banana
First President of Zimbabwe

Entrepreneur
MAGAZINE

Rieva Lesonsky
Vice President
Editor in Chief

SUCCESS

Success, to me, is embodied by the late great New York Yankees outfielder Mickey Mantle. Mickey Mantle hit 536 homeruns in his lifetime.   Indeed he is remembered as a homerun hitter. But he also struck out 1,710 times.

Every time Mantle went to the plate, he had the same chance to do either. Yet, he kept going to the plate and swinging for those fences. As his record indicates, sometimes he connected; more often he didn't.

But as Robert Kennedy once said, "Only those who dare to fail miserably can achieve greatly."

Success means daring to fail -- a lesson we all can learn.

Sincerely,

Rieva Lesonsky
Vice President/Editor in Chief
ENTREPRENEUR MAGAZINE

Rieva Lesonsky
Vice President and Editor in Chief, *Entrepreneur Magazine*

Sir James R. Mancham KBE

24 July 1996

Thank you for your letter of 3rd May 1996 inviting me to contribute a quote, story, poem or personal experience which defines "success".

In my view, however rich a man becomes or however much he accomplishes, he is not to be regarded as successful if his fame or wealth costs him his "Peace of Mind". I would like therefore to contribute what I wrote on the subject in a little book I published in 1989 entitled, *Peace of Mind*.

You can publish this with due credit to me and I look forward to receive a complimentary copy of your finished publication in the not-too-distant future.

With best regards.

Yours sincerely

Sir James R Mancham, KBE

James R. Mancham
President of Seychelles

Quote:

"Tell us, my soul, about the richest man in the world.
Well I found him on a small island in the Micronesian archipelago
beaming a two-billion-dollar smile under a coconut palm.
He had never seen any pictures of the world beyond his shores
and was consequently not bothered about the problem of "rising
expectations."
Food and water were not in abundance—
Every day he had to fish to feed his family and collect water
from a well on the other side of the island.
These conditions provided him with a challenge each morning
and "job satisfaction" at the end of every day.

For music, he listened to the murmur of the waves,
The songs of the birds and the occasional thunder from above.
He had no master paintings to look at
Save the ones which are created by the Supreme Master around
his island every day.
Every sunrise and sunset was a work of art *par excellence*
And in the evening, instead of watching the T.V.,
He contemplated the sky, the stars and the moon
By virtue of which process he communicated with the Lord his
Master
And gave thanks to him to be alive.
He paid no taxes, had never heard about insurance companies
nor pensions schemes.
Nor had he ever dreamt about a will—or death duties.
He was just a "happy" and "contented" man with "peace of mind."

There are many people with millions in the banks today
But with no smiles on their faces because
Neither Harrods, nor Lonrho, nor the International Division of
Sothebys Parke Burnett
Has ever been able to put for sale "Peace of Mind."

(Published by JRM International—London)

James R. Mancham
President of Seychelles

Richard M. DeVos

August 16, 1996

I'm happy to provide you with the following quote:

> For many years, I've been telling audiences about a philosophy of success
> that I call "The Three A's: Action, Attitude, and Atmosphere." Successful
> people are raised in an atmosphere or choose to live in an atmosphere of
> positive people who tell them they can do it. They have a can-do attitude
> and believe they can achieve their dreams. Most important, they take
> action to fulfill their dreams of success. They go ahead and try something
> instead of fearing failure and never trying anything.
>
> True success is not measured by wealth or material possessions. Success
> is really about achievement and using your God-given talents to reach
> whatever goals you have in life. Once we succeed, our responsibility is to
> tell others that they can do it, too, and to give them hope. If we don't use
> our success to help others achieve, we've failed in our mission.

Sincerely,

Richard M. DeVos
Co-Founder and Former President
Amway Corporation

Richard M. DeVos
Cofounder and Former President, Amway Corporation

STATE OF NEBRASKA

EXECUTIVE SUITE
P.O. Box 94848
Lincoln, Nebraska 68509-4848
Phone (402) 471-2244

E. Benjamin Nelson
Governor

To achieve success, I believe one must set goals and priorities. I set a goal of being Governor when I was a teenager, and it remained a goal throughout my careers in law and the insurance industry. No matter where I was in my life, my priorities have always been family first, then getting things done in the best way possible.

I also believe truly successful people are those who give back to their communities, states and countries. I see my role as a public servant as a way to help people and to make a difference.

E. Benjamin Nelson
Governor of Nebraska

E. Benjamin Nelson
Governor of Nebraska

Ten Words for Marriage

by shirley Jones

THREE YEARS AGO, on our tenth anniversary, I made up a special greeting card for Marty, which turned out to be much more than a Hallmark wish. It has stayed with me, and with him, for all this time. It not only sits in a special place that I can call upon when we lose our way some, I often share it with anyone who feels a cloud passing over their home.

It is *The Ten-Word Manual for Marriage*. We learned it one word a year. Maybe we can save you some time.

1. <u>TRUTH</u>   The only way to go, with anything, especially love. And there is absolutely no defense against it; it is the purest communication there is. Try it, with yourself first, then with your person. Work on it. It will lift all the weight off your shoulders.

2. <u>STRATEGIES</u>   These are the learned disasters we brought from high school; produced only by fear and insecurity. Builds only walls between you. Makes strangers of people you thought you knew. Enemy of truth and sincerity and everything permanent. Dump them.

3. <u>HUMOR</u>   Easier said than done, but do it, find it, feel it, look for partners with it. Life's absurd as it is. Try laughing at it. Just make the *sound* first. It's contagious, and medicinal, and addictive.

4. <u>REPRESSION</u>   The *real* cancer of our time. And an irresistible trap. "Suck it in." "Save it." "It'll go away." *No, no, no.* It never does. It just rumbles and simmers till the big quake. Repress *nothing*, neither the sweet nor the bitter. Let it out, no matter how unsettling. *Today's small eruption is better than tomorrow's doomsday!*

Shirley Jones
Actress

5. <u>VULNERABILITY</u> It's a *virtue*. Big one. Trust me. But it's hard. (You'll feel like you're the world's number-one target.) Not so. Start. Open up. It's lovable, it's disarming, and it's courageous.

6. <u>SELF-ESTEEM</u> The magic words. If you won't muster any for you, nobody else will. And it's like Western Union: If you don't have any, they all get the message. Any spare time, work on liking yourself better. It'll put a new paint job on everything.

7. <u>CHANGE</u> There's always someone to tell you you have to. *Wrong. Don't.* Rather, spend the time finding out who you *really are*. Work on being more of *that*. A lot better than the futile "gotta-change" treadmill, which really never ends.

8. <u>SPACE</u> A lover's most precious gift. Most of us don't offer it, for fear of losing control. Fight that. Find the guts to hand some out, the kind you'd like for yourself. Don't be afraid to trust it. It can only make you look better, and be loved more for it.

9. <u>FRIENDS</u> Terribly overlooked "balance" for a twosome. And necessary: Make sure your "mutual" ones include some from *both* sides. (One-sided friend lists, no matter how intriguing or comfortable, invariably mean trouble down the road.)

10. <u>PRIVACY</u> Save some for the both of you, no matter how pressing your commitments. Be alone together. Talk, touch, stare, think, read, but do it with the world on the other side of the door. It's not only healthy, it'll "test" what you've got.

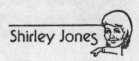

Shirley Jones

Shirley Jones
Actress

DEPARTMENT OF AGRICULTURE
OFFICE OF THE SECRETARY
WASHINGTON, D.C. 20250

June 2 5 1996

I am pleased to enclose a copy of my "Secretary's Column" that was recently published by the Office of Communications entitled *Gleaning and Food Rescue -- A Message from the Secretary.*

Thanks again for your request. I hope this information is helpful.

Sincerely,

DAN GLICKMAN
Secretary

Dan Glickman
U.S. Secretary of Agriculture

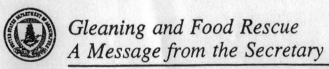

Gleaning and Food Rescue
A Message from the Secretary

U.S. Department of Agriculture
Office of Communications

Feeding the Hungry
By Agriculture Secretary Dan Glickman

When I was a boy and left food on my plate, my mother would say, "Think of all the poor starving children in Asia." Those poor, starving children are right here in the United States, too.

The latest census figures show there were 38.1 million Americans in poverty last year -- half of them children or senior citizens. Nearly one in four children lives in poverty, and the United States ranks 24th among all nations in its infant mortality rate. Requests for emergency food are increasing and the need cannot be met.

We must be creative and find new ways to get food to people who need it, especially in times of budgetary restraint, in times when some are trying to unravel the social safety net.

Billy Shore, founder of the anti-hunger organization Share Our Strength, said recently, "Instead of being shocking, poverty has become mind-numbingly routine."

He's right. We have become insensitive to the sight of the homeless on our streets and the poor children in our schools. And Congress is beginning to say we should leave their care to the saints and the Good Samaritans.

I want to emphasize that USDA's food and nutrition assistance programs, such as the food stamp and school lunch programs, are essential for the nation's poor and hungry and must be protected. But even with federal assistance and the work of charities and nonprofit organizations, the needs of the poor and hungry exceed the supply.

However, there is one source of food already available if we can learn to use it better.

It has been estimated that nearly one-fifth of all the food produced for human consumption in this country is lost every year -- in fields, commercial kitchens, markets, stores, schools and restaurants. Healthful, uneaten food is often thrown away and is not saved or recycled for future use. We have to find ways to get that surplus food into the mouths of the hungry before it goes into the mouth of the dumpster. So USDA is leading a national effort to coordinate public and private efforts to rescue this food.

The practice of gleaning -- gathering after the reapers -- is not new. A passage in Leviticus reads: "When you reap the harvest of your land, do not reap the corners of your field,

Dan Glickman
U.S. Secretary of Agriculture

and do not glean the fallen ears of your crop ... you must leave them for the poor and the stranger."

Because it is one of my highest personal priorities as Secretary, I will host a conference this month in Washington on food rescue. I want to bring together government, businesses, workers, and the nonprofit community to see how we can alleviate some of our nation's hunger problems through creative gleaning projects.

I am not interested in creating major new government program bureaucracies. I am interested in developing partnerships with the private sector and nonprofit community to look for ways to facilitate food distribution at the local level.

Much is already being done in both the public and private sectors, in big cities and small towns:

- Each Friday, 150 pounds of food from USDA's cafeteria goes to the DC Central Kitchen, a non-profit organization that serves shelters and soup kitchens all over Washington. If all federal departments and agencies donate their cafeteria's leftover food, it would be more than 1,000 pounds each week.

- Foodchain, a network of 130 food-rescue programs across the United States and Canada, collects surplus prepared and perishable foods for distribution to the hungry. Last year, Foodchain programs helped feed more than 183,000 hungry people every day.

The Los Angeles Charitable Food Distribution Center's dock at the L.A. Wholesale Produce Market offers about 300 charities produce that is not in salable condition but is still perfectly good to eat and is donated by wholesalers at the market.

The nation's linen industry is helping feed the hungry. Operation Food Share organizes linen service companies, their food service customers, and local hunger agencies for food rescue. Hunger agencies supply containers to linen services whose food service customers fill the containers with unserved, excess food, which is labeled and frozen. Linen service sales representatives pick up full containers and leave empty ones during normal deliveries.

And there is a need for more than food. Food rescue operations need refrigerated trucks, food-storage supplies, and office equipment. UPS Foundation, for example, provides reduced-rate refrigerated trucks and low-rate maintenance on vehicles to food rescue programs.

Much is being done. But we can -- and must -- do more.

We need your ideas, your creative solutions to this problem. We want to know how we can work with local communities. We want to hear what you're doing that works and then replicate it elsewhere. So let us hear from you: Office of Intergovernmental Affairs, Room 219A, U.S. Department of Agriculture, 14th and Independence SW, Washington, DC 20250, (Fax: 202-720--8819).

We have a special obligation in America to make sure that no one ever goes to bed hungry. It makes a good New Year's resolution.

Dan Glickman
U.S. Secretary of Agriculture

Not everyone will achieve the kind of success bestowed from outside oneself. The other, more meaningful, success is defined from within and is not measured in terms of wealth, power, or fame. It does not always come easily and, in many instances, only after some failure. Then it becomes even more precious. To me, success is the sense of self-fulfillment and satisfaction derived from doing something you love and doing it to the best of your ability. And if, on occasion, you transcend your ability and achieve something you thought impossible, then you experience true success.

Seiji Ozawa
Music Director
Boston Symphony Orchestra

Seiji Ozawa
Music Director, Boston Symphony Orchestra

"When you're at your limit and your goal seems impossible, a little more work, patience and positive thinking may lead you to the satisfaction of achievement."

Peter Carruthers
1984 Olympic Silver Medalist

Peter Carruthers
Olympic Silver-Medal Figure Skater

monty hall

To some people success is measured in terms of
money or fame. While those achievements cannot
be overlooked, I like to measure success by
evaluating my life, my contributions to society,
my family and my friends. I have been blessed
with a wonderful wife, three outstanding and
achieving children, and three gorgeous
grandchildren. Through my charitable work in
Canada and the United States, I have seen
hospitals built, camps erected for handicapped
children and research performed for so many
diseases.

My father defined my success thusly, "do not talk
to me of my son the T.V. star - talk to me of my
son the humanitarian." When your father defines
you life in that manner - that is success!

Monty Hall
Television Personality

When I was a child, I used to think it wrong to pray for anything specific, so I only prayed that I would be happy. I have a friend who says that if one manages to be happy he has lived a successful life. In a recent newspaper interview, a serial killer was asked why he committed the unprovoked murders. "It made me happy," he responded. He, of course, and even those who devote their lives to seemingly harmless pursuits, are not necessarily a success in my eyes. The purpose of life is not just to be happy..

At my grandson's high school commencement ceremonies, the valedictorian began his address talking of his father who had died when he was a child. He described him as an ordinary person who had never achieved fame, fortune or rank, and, in the eyes of the world, not a success. Our speaker went on to describe his relationship with his father and attributed the fact that he was making this address as valedictorian to his father's influence and inspiration. His conclusion was that if an individual affects in a positive fashion, even one individual, his life has been a success.

This young man's moving address spoke my definition of success. The person whose life positively affects another, whether through a direct relationship or indirectly, is glorifying God.

But living a life which helps another can bring happiness. A Hindu proverb says, "Help thy brother's boat across and lo! Thine own has reach the shore!"

Happy sailing!

Caroline Rose Hunt

Caroline Rose Hunt

Caroline Rose Hunt
Founder and President, Lady Primrose's Royal Bathing Luxuries

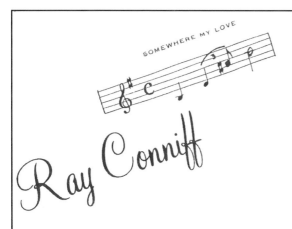

If you had your choice for a lifetime activity, what would it be?

OK ..... THEN DO IT!

Ray Conniff
Ray Conniff

Ray Conniff
Conductor/Composer

ROBERT L. SHAPIRO
Attorney at Law

A PROFESSIONAL CORPORATION

KAREN FILIPI
MEMBER CALIF. AND N. J. BARS
SARA L. CAPLAN
MEMBER CALIF. AND MICH. BARS

November 2, 1995

Thank you for your letter of October 24, 1995 requesting my participation in your research project to benefit The Make-A-Wish Foundation.

Your thought-provoking question -- What is my personal definition of success? -- is challenging, to say the least. The very fact that you have solicited my opinion implies a certain degree of success in itself, and I am honored to oblige you and The Make-A-Wish Foundation.

Success is a state of mind, I think. The personal triumphs that one achieves as a result of his or her own efforts are many times more valuable than the accidental attainment of any prize. When we master a musical instrument or a foreign language, for example, we bask in the satisfaction of accomplishment. True success is an "A" on a child's report card, an athlete's personal best, the will to break a bad habit. Success, to me, means winning my own approval.

Thank you again for inviting me to participate. I wish you great *success* with this project.

Sincerely,

ROBERT L. SHAPIRO

Robert L. Shapiro
Attorney

JACK LEMMON

November 16, 1995

The biggest problem in defining success, in my opinion, is that people too often think of success in terms of other people's opinion. I don't think that a person is "successful" merely because he has made a fortune, or because he is a household word, or because other people consider him to be a success.

Rather, I think success must be one's own opinion of one's self. If a person strives to be a truly decent human being, and in his or her professional endeavors tries basically to accomplish goals as well as he or she possibly can, then that person could be considered extremely successul. I do not think striving to be "the best in the world" at anything is realistic or desirable. (In acting, for instance, there is no such thing as the "best" actor in the world. And striving to be that is ridiculous. One's goal as an actor--like all other professions-- should be to be the best that one can be, and above all to make sure that I don't hurt anybody else in the process of my endeavors.)

Obviously, I feel that personal success is intimately involved with self-esteem, and I do not think that one can define success without involving self-esteem.

I hope that these thoughts are of help to you.

Most sincerely,

Jack Lemmon

Jack Lemmon
Actor

GLORIA LORING

December 4, 1995

My definition of success is the following:

"I believe that a successful life is one that springs from the deep intuition of the heart - finding a passion, a calling that not only fulfills our dreams, but leads us to be of service to family, friend, and community. Once that calling is clear, true success lies in living with kindness and respect as constant companions in all one's undertakings."

Good luck with your project.

Sincerely,

Gloria Loring

Gloria Loring
Actress

December 05, 1995

This is in response to you letter of November 10th, inviting me to provide you with a quote, story, etc. which defines success to me written on my personal stationary. Unfortunately, as far as the latter, the computer is my personal stationary. As far as the former, I am honored, but I have no idea which of the many words I've heard or events I've experienced define success. However, the following are some thoughts along the line which I hope will be adequate:

Every morning, before the start of homeroom class, my fifth grade teacher, Mrs. Bishop, made us recite "Good, better, best. Never let it rest, until the good is better and the better is best." I thought it was one of the dumbest things I had ever heard and hated reciting it.

My father, not at all a successful man financially, but a very good numbers writer and bookie, told me "Do whatever you want in life, as long as you don't hurt the other guy." I had no idea what he was talking about, especially living in a slum environment in which a lot of people were always hurting someone.

My mother told me "David, you are very special and can accomplish whatever you set out to do in life, but just make certain, whatever it is, you are happy." I loved the vote of confidence but was confused by the happiness part.

When I was thirteen years old, I said to my mother "I'm shooting for the highest star up there, Mom, because, if I miss, the worse that'll happen is I'll fall onto the moon, but if I aim only for the moon and miss, I'm liable to land right back in the neighborhood." I understood what I meant, but had no idea how to achieve it.

I reached that star. I achieved success. What is my definition of it and how did I accomplish it? I guess all the above words I heard and then some. All I can truly tell you is that it was worth everything that had to be done to achieve it; I didn't hurt the other guy and I am happy.

David Brenner

David Brenner
Comedian

Knowing I've made a difference in someone's life, seeing a face light up with joy, feeling my hand pressed warmly, hearing, "Oh, may I PLEASE hug you, girl? You make me laugh SO HARD!"

Then I knew that, however bumblingly, I'm succeeding.

— Rue McClanahan
~ Away from home
with no
stationery ~

Rue McClanahan
Actress

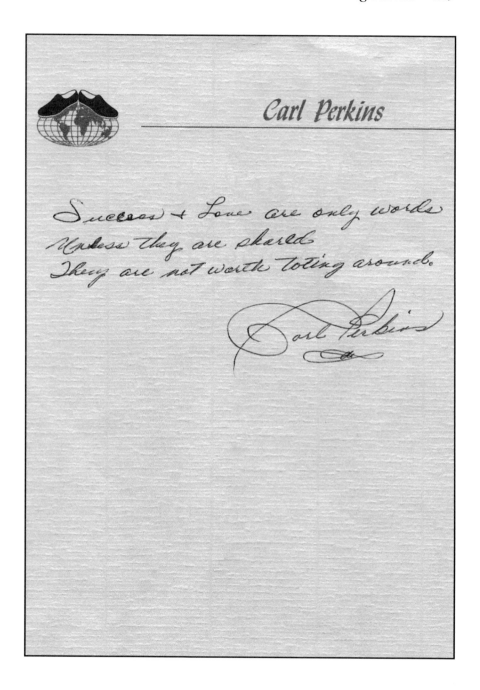

Carl Perkins

Success + Love are only words
Unless they are shared
They are not worth toting around.

Carl Perkins

Carl Perkins
Singer

A MAGYAR KÖZTÁRSASÁG
ELNÖKÉNEK HIVATALA
1641/GA/R24/95

Budapest, December 8, 1995

Referring to your letter addressed to the President of the Republic of Hungary I have the pleasure to send you the definition of success by His Excellency:

"The success is the ability to enforce the talent for the prosperity - and not to the detriment - of the community"

I wish you every success,

Sincerely yours,

Zsolt Rábai
Foreign Policy Adviser
to the President

Arpad Goncz
President of Hungary

Art Linkletter

November 7, 1995

Defining success is a complex task. It is a slippery slope when you think of success in all its many guises: wealth, power, and fame. My own concept of success has to put happiness first, and that, too, has multiple meanings, depending upon the culture and the individual. No one can be truly successful in my opinion who doesn't have a happy life. No one can be happy who has squandered his health. No one can be truly happy unless he has acquired a positive attitude towards his associates, his career, and his outlook on life.

After health, I consider attitude to be the element in success that must be developed. A career is not truly successful unless it is enjoyed. Getting up in the morning each day and feeling good about what you do and are going to do is paramount.

Because success is not a destination; it is a journey.

I hope this will help.

Cordially,

Art Linkletter
Speaker/Television Personality

19th May 1996.

The details of your letter concerning your project to define -Successful Living, leaves me some what in a puzzler, for the very word Success seems to me no yard stick for anything. The only gift we have is life itself, & Love & to work with serious endeavour.

Since we are all so very small indeed, so our love does not have to be lofty - even a little is an enormous contribution. For my part I was inspired by a painting I saw, in what was at that time devastation & desperation, when I was a child, all I knew then is what I know now is that there is a life to discover in painting, & that one painting leads to another.

Yours sincerely

David Tindle

David Tindle
Artist

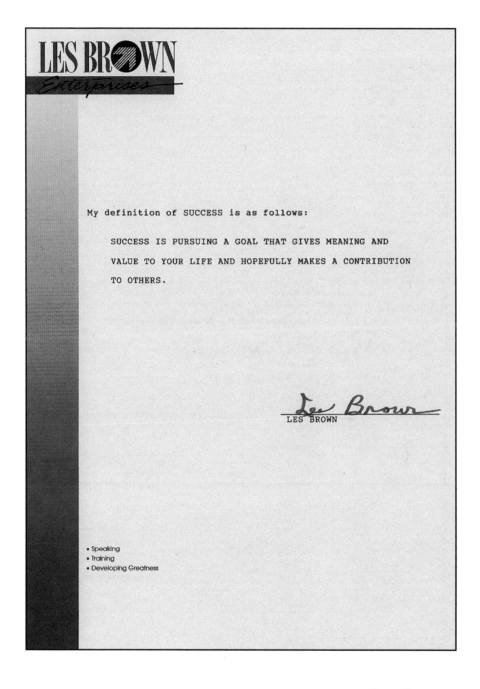

My definition of SUCCESS is as follows:

    SUCCESS IS PURSUING A GOAL THAT GIVES MEANING AND

    VALUE TO YOUR LIFE AND HOPEFULLY MAKES A CONTRIBUTION

    TO OTHERS.

LES BROWN

Les Brown
Author/Motivational Speaker

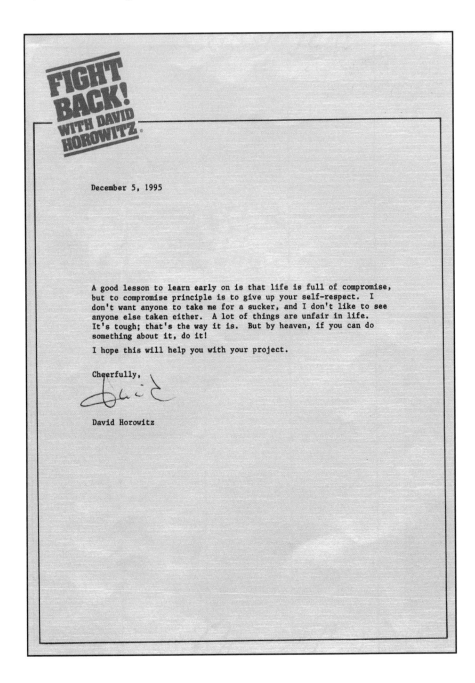

FIGHT BACK! WITH DAVID HOROWITZ

December 5, 1995

A good lesson to learn early on is that life is full of compromise, but to compromise principle is to give up your self-respect. I don't want anyone to take me for a sucker, and I don't like to see anyone else taken either. A lot of things are unfair in life. It's tough; that's the way it is. But by heaven, if you can do something about it, do it!

I hope this will help you with your project.

Cheerfully,

David Horowitz

David Horowitz
Commentator/Consumer Advocate

CHILDREN OF THE NIGHT

Recipient of the "1984 President's Volunteer Action Award"

November 16, 1995

"Success is working at something you really believe in and immensely enjoy. No matter how hard you work, you look forward to the day ahead and go to sleep at night thinking about how much more needs to be done the following day. This does not mean that your work is not difficult or frustrating sometimes, but that you enjoy it every single day and feel that you are accomplishing something really important."

Sincerely,

Lois Lee

Dr. Lois Lee

Lois Lee
Founder, Children of the Night

GOUVERNEUR
VAN DE
NEDERLANDSE ANTILLEN

True success lies in the showing of a personal, positive and humane approach to others and obstacles, and in causing the basic values to flourish concretely in our own lives and in the lives of others. We should make a realistic commitment to a harmonious set of purposes, and should look only for opportunities and not for difficulties and obstacles.

The Governor-General of the Netherlands Antilles

Dr Jaime M. Saleh

Jaime M. Saleh
Governor-General of the Netherlands Antilles

Success is won by NOT seeking it.
Using discipline, dedication and
diligence to reach a specific
goal — without wavering off course
or even a slight doubt that the
journey will not be reached —
will result automatically in
Success.   Success, not money,
can be the goal.   The goal
must be to win at the target set.
Success and money are the
reward — and with it comes
peace, satisfaction and contentment —
when it is not sought! Go enjoy
Success bigtime.

Robin Leach
Television Personality and Producer

VICTORIA TENNANT

Someone who perceived me to be successful, "because of personal accomplishment, fame or wealth" asked me to write something inspirational about success. Well, here I am, trying to sort out what the word "success" means to me. I suppose that within the definition applied to me there are two kinds of success, one coming from personal accomplishment, the other from fame or wealth. Fame or wealth achieved without accomplishment is not what we are talking about so let's forget about them, and if they come as a result of real accomplishment let's also forget about them because that's putting the cart before the horse.

So, that leaves us with "personal accomplishment". Is a private personal accomplishment worth less than a public one which might result in fame and wealth? Many people would say, yes. But what use is accomplishment if it doesn't bring a measure of happiness and peace of mind? I know for sure that fame and wealth do not necessarily bring those things; what they do bring is the privilege of being as troubled as everybody else in comfort. I agree, that is something, that's why I say it's a privilege, but to be troubled in comfort is not really inspiring as a goal in life.

There are many gifted people who were never recognised publicly, and many who were by chance, many who were recognised in old age after a lifetime of excellent work, and many only after their deaths. So the only thing we can depend on is knowing within ourselves whether we have accomplished something or not. A private sense of accomplishment. We know if we have done a job well, we know no matter what anyone else tells us, and only we know if we succeeded in overcoming obstacles within ourselves to do it or if it was easy. We know if we are being the best we can be, or at least trying, and that seems to me to be a worthwhile goal.

In fact trying to be the best you can be is what a really accomplished person does, all the time. Being the best you can be happens sometimes if you try a lot, it just comes over you, you rise to a higher level of ability for a moment or for a while or forever. Trying to be the best that you can be, all the time is hard, because you never know when you will be rewarded for all that effort, and the answer is that the trying has to be part of the reward in itself.

If you are the best person that you can be, that is the most that you can do. You may have a gift that is a part of you, a gift for singing or acting, teaching or nursing, painting or dancing, gardening or cooking, playing sports or doing business, but that should be a part of you, a part of the big picture. Often the talent takes over and someone becomes the best at doing something and forgets about being a good person. It's difficult to keep one's balance when the outside world makes such a big deal about outside things and doesn't honour the private ones.

Honour yourself. Honour yourself and those you love. Honour the world around you and the people around you and whatever you do. Find a place in your life for peace, for grace, and a place in your heart for compassion and forgiveness. If you do, you may make it easier for love to find you and become a part of you. And that is the one accomplishment that to me means anything at all.

Victoria Tennant

Victoria Tennant
Actress

September 13, 1996

The following is *"Robb Report's"* definition of success:

"Success does not just mean achieving one's goals and the attainment of great possessions. It also means having the time to savor them as well. In this day and age, free time itself may now be the ultimate measure of success."

Sincerely,

ROBB REPORT INC.

Tracy L. Phillips
Publisher

Tracy L. Phillips
Publisher, *Robb Report Magazine*

Make-A-Wish Foundation®
of America

September 26, 1996

Every day at the Make-A-Wish Foundation, we are privileged to bear witness to a powerful, non-traditional reality of success. When children come to us, they're taking the first step toward successes of a much simpler, more profound and urgent nature than we are accustomed to realizing in our everyday lives.

When we enter the lives of these special children, nothing in life is going their way. For sick youngsters, the usual childhood rituals of family, friends, school and the process of maturity are frantically replaced with a regimen of doctor visits and often painful medical therapies. Discomfort and sadness come, though they've done nothing wrong. These children lose control of their happiness, their dignity, their unyielding spirit simply to be children. The traumatic nature of their illnesses sometimes segregate them from the daily lives of their healthier friends and family members, and the preoccupation with trying to work through life one week at a time robs them of their ability to dream of life beyond their next treatment.

Our role in children's lives is to grant their special, unique wish. The wish experience gives these children the permission to think about the future - to plan for that trip to Disney World, to meet that celebrity. To be, simply and innocently, happy.

When a child makes a wish to us - "I wish I could visit my grandparents" or "I wish I could have a computer" - our network of volunteers, staff and donors move mountains to make that wish come true. Then we stand back, deeply moved and ever humbled, as we watch the children rise up and take back control of a piece of their lives. Where they cannot wish their painful diseases away, they **can** wish that joy, smiles and life be breathed back into them and their families. They, not their disease, choose their reality, if only for a day. This empowerment brings them a moment of joy and peace -- on their terms.

Success! Mom and Dad laughed again. My pain went away, for awhile. No needles today. No blood tests. Pure fun. Sweet success. To some children and their families, the fulfillment of a wish provides the long sought-for peace and happiness in their lives.

It did to April. She was a homeless Seattle teenager in the final stages of a blood disease who knew that doctors had given her only about four days to live when she received a call from Make-A-Wish. "You know I'm only going to be around for a few more days," she reminded the Make-A-Wish volunteers. It was two weeks before Christmas, and she had no wish for herself. Her wish was for the wish-granters to shop for other homeless children so they would be happy on Christmas. That made sense to her. It would be her legacy. It was her fondest wish. And when she was presented a videotape of a Make-A-Wish volunteer playing Santa Claus to a jubilant

Stephen E. Torkelsen
President and CEO, Make-A-Wish Foundation

crowd of squealing children at a Seattle homeless shelter, she cried with the satisfaction of witnessing her dream become reality. When the cards, letters and donations to homeless children came in from around the country, she was there to acknowledge them - and enjoy her own success. April, who had only days to live when Make-A-Wish called, lived in the warm glow of her dream for nine more months.

Recently we watched in awe as 4-year-old Robin, his grown-up mind hard at work inside his tiny body, outwitted a hospital full of diseases for a day. He is fighting leukemia, and he lives in Houston - mostly at the Texas Children's Hospital. Robin's wish was, in his words, "to be the boss of the ice cream man." Why? So he could make sure his friends at the hospital and the kids in his neighborhood back home, could have all the ice cream they wanted. A child's ideal of happiness - to laugh, play and enjoy an ice cream cone with your buddies - came to life. Robin succeeded in bringing joy both to the pensive environment of the children's hospital, and to children in his neighborhood who may have missed having him around as a playmate. A truckload of ice cream, served by volunteers, was the instrument to bring joy and life. A success. All because of Robin.

Recently we learned that success sometimes has a melodic sound. This time, it took on an unmistakably country-western tone. Kevin was a standout athlete in Sacramento who dreamed of becoming a country music singer when he was diagnosed with bone cancer at age 17. Not sure whether he would ever have the chance to realize his dream of being a professional singer, Kevin made a wish to meet legendary country music producer David Foster. The two struck up a friendship that neither was sure would last very long. But as Kevin was drawn into the wonder of the music business and all its possibilities, he found the strength to continue fighting the disease aggressively because his wish of being a musician gave him a plan for his life. Today he's 25. His cancer is in remission. He's just cut his first country album. A national tour is in the works. Also, he has a special song you should hear.

Make-A-Wish grants a wish somewhere in America on the average of every 90 minutes. We are often praised for the joy and happiness we bring into the lives of seriously ill children. But I don't see that as our success. Our success is the child's success. Every 90 minutes, a new ray of hope reaches out to an ill child. Every 90 minutes, another child is freed to be a child again, or to dare to think about their own unique future, without costs or limits. We as service people at Make-A-Wish live vicariously through their powerful journeys, and we learn from the simple eloquence of their examples how we might reexamine the qualities we use to measure success in our own lives: joy, peace, dignity, and happiness shared.

Sincerely,

Stephen Torkelsen

Stephen E. Torkelsen, DSW
President and Chief Executive Officer
Make-A-Wish Foundation of America.

Stephen E. Torkelsen
President and CEO, Make-A-Wish Foundation

ROBERT SCHULLER

REACH OUT FOR NEW LIFE

"My Definition of Success"
by Robert H. Schuller

I have a simple definition of success:

Success is building self-esteem in yourself and others through sincere service.

We could say: Success is self-respect. It's that wonderful feeling that comes to you when you have helped others help themselves to a better and more beautiful life.

Now we see why success is so important.   Because the alternative is failure, and failure is disastrous to a person's self-esteem. Without a successful experience, you will remain trapped in the impoverished ghetto of a negative self-image.   Success turns you around from being a non-loving person into a positive person with healthy self-love.

All Supersuccessful People know that self-esteem is life's highest value. They know the joy of getting is being able to give to those in need. They know the joy of sharing the fruits of success. This great joy is the experience of self-esteem. So building self-esteem in yourself is both the motive and the measure of success.

That's why I challenge you to get set and join the Supersuccess circle. Whoever you are, wherever you are, I invite you to climb the success ladder, all the way to the top.

Regardless of the circumstances!

Sincerely,

Robert H. Schuller

Robert H. Schuller
Religious Leader

"Success is looking in the mirror and seeing a worthy role model for the children of the world to emulate."

Wishing you all the best,

Dr. Denis Waitley

Denis Waitley
Author/Motivational Speaker

Walters Speaker Services
• Walters International Speakers Bureau • Royal Publishing • "Sharing Ideas" Newsmagazine

Dottie Walters
President

Monday, November 18, 1996

Definition of success.

I believe that success is to fulfill the mission we were entrusted with at the moment we were conceived.

Of all the myriad possibilities of genes, we each are the unique combination of possibilities the Creator envisioned at our creation. If I have helped others, loved all who came in contact with me, used my talents to their upmost so that they grew as seeds do into strong plants with flowers and fruit, then my mission here is complete.

Two of my many dear friends of the mind said it best:
  Ralph Waldo Emerson, "The creation of a thousand forests is in one acorn."
  Lao Tsze: "To see things in the seed that is genius."

Dottie Walters, International Speaker, Author, Consultant
President, Walters International Speakers Bureau
Publisher/Editor, SHARING IDEAS NEWSMAGAZINE

Dottie Walters
Author/Speaker

Harvey B. Mackay
Chief Executive Officer

Nov. 5, 1996

Success

by Harvey Mackay

"Success is:

1) the name of the magazine;

2) getting paid for doing what you like to do;

3) falling in love with your spouse;

4) being able to stop worrying about yourself and start caring about others;

5) having a grandchild say, 'I love you';

6) when 'they' think you're so successful, they ask you to define 'success.'"

Harvey Mackay

Harvey B. Mackay
Businessman/Author

ROBERT GOULET
President

VERA GOULET
Vice President

From the desk of
ROBERT GOULET

11/9/95

As I was never a huge seller of recordings and never had my own television show— and never made a dent in films, I guess you could say that success has eluded me.

Yet, at the age of 62, I'm still hanging in there.

Perhaps my father's last words to me on his deathbed, "God gave you a voice, you must sing!" proved to be the catalyst that urged me on.

Robert Goulet
Singer/Actor

ROGO & ROVE

ROBERT GOULET
President

VERA GOULET
Vice President

From the desk of
ROBERT GOULET

I find success in the smiles on the faces of those in the audience.

I find it in their applause and in the letters they send.

That alone should keep any performer humming.

One should always remember that "Success — is in the eye of the beholder!"

Robert Goulet

Robert Goulet
Singer/Actor

If you're happy about what
you do in your life,
you've already achieved
the ultimate success.

Wyland

Wyland
Artist

SUCCESSORIES

Ideas For Positive People

My definition of success . . .

As we know, success means many things to many people, but I feel that one of

our bestselling posters, entitled **Priorities**, puts everything into perspective. It

says: "A hundred years from now it will not matter what my bank account

was, the sort of house I lived in, or the kind of car I drove . . . but the world may

be different because I was important in the life of a child."

Mac Anderson
Chairman and CEO

Mac Anderson
Chairman and CEO, Successories

William E. Bailey

Founder of Bestline Products and Heratio Alger Award Recipient

Success

Success is when you can live each day filled with the joy and zest of living. It is receiving spiritual rewards, physical rewards, the rewards of having loving relationships with family and friends, and financial rewards because of the value you bring to the lives of others. That is success.

William E. Bailey

William E. Bailey

William E. Bailey
Businessman/Horatio Alger Award Recipient

Jim Rohn International

Sales • Management • Personal Development

Success

Success is neither magical nor mysterious. Success is the natural consequence of a few simple disciplines, practiced every day, while failure is simply a few errors in judgment, repeated every day.   It is the accumulative weight of our disciplines and our judgments that leads us to either fortune or failure.

Jim Rohn

Jim Rohn
Author/Motivational Speaker

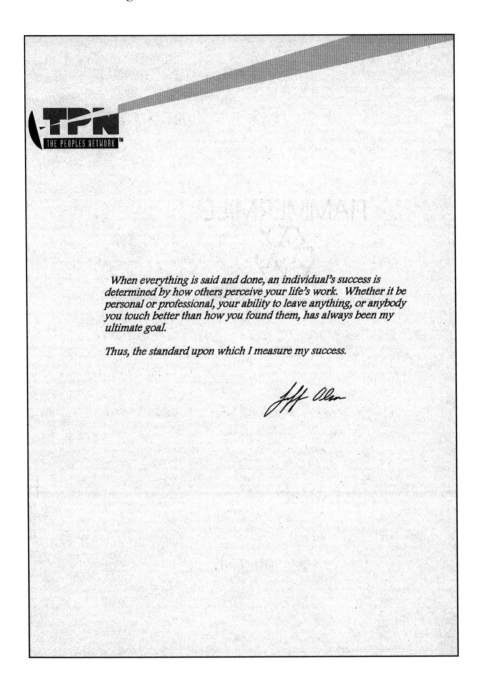

When everything is said and done, an individual's success is determined by how others perceive your life's work. Whether it be personal or professional, your ability to leave anything, or anybody you touch better than how you found them, has always been my ultimate goal.

Thus, the standard upon which I measure my success.

Jeff Olson
Founder, President and CEO, The Peoples Network

SCOTT DeGARMO
EDITOR IN CHIEF & PUBLISHER

Success means having a heartfelt goal and working to achieve it.

The moment we commit ourselves to attaining our highest objectives, we become successful in the way that matters most.

If we don't accomplish our mission, our attempts may be noted as failures in the eyes of others. However, from our own perspective, these efforts are just learning experiences. The only true failure is the result of not trying.

For me, observing the successes of others is a source of never-ending amazement and inspiration. Whenever I am tempted to quit, I think about the examples of courage, tenacity, and healthy ambition by people in every walk of life, past and present, and I am quickly inspired to return to the struggle with renewed energy.

Scott DeGarmo
Publisher, *Success Magazine*

HERBALIFE.

MARK HUGHES
President and Founder
Chief Executive Officer

I believe that success begins the minute you start working toward your goals. The actions you take to fulfill your dreams and attain your personal desires make you a success today, not the end results you will get tomorrow.

While success is in your actions, it is also in the way you choose to act. So decide what is meaningful to you and then pursue it with integrity, virtue, humility and most importantly, good will toward people. I always treat others with the utmost respect they deserve. It does not matter what someone's background is, their job title, where they reside, what car they drive, how much or how little education they have, or the dollar figure they earn. That's not what defines a person...their character does.

I approach everyone I meet with the attitude that we are all winners and can make a huge difference in this world. By believing in someone else's unique qualities and encouraging them to strive for personal excellence, I am helping them start their personal journey of success. I do not think you can ever be satisfied with your own success unless you teach others how to accomplish it as well. Teaching the gift of action is really teaching someone how to turn dreams into reality. And, our dreams weave the fabric that connects us all together.

When I was 16 years old, I knew I wanted to make a difference in the world. I had no idea what it would be our how I would accomplish this task, but I was determined to affect people's lives in a positive way. As a result of a personal tragedy, I became impassioned about nutrition. In 1980, I started Herbalife International and dedicated my life to spreading the message of good health through advanced nutrition around the world. I didn't reach the four corners of the globe in my first day of business, so I got up the next morning and tried it again. Day after day, week after week, year after year of hard work, commitment and dedication to my dream has turned it into a reality of which I am extremely proud. What I have discovered in 17 years is that every small step I have taken has contributed to the giant strides I have made in helping to vastly improve people's lives.

Of course, I have had my share of business ups and downs, but I've learned to equally appreciate the good *and* difficult times because both situations offer me the opportunity to do better and greater things. No matter how tough the challenge is before me, I never give up and that's an essential ingredient for personal success. So hang in there. Stay on course. Persevere. Carry on. Weather the storm. If you do, you will fully understand the meaning of success!

Mark Hughes

Mark Hughes
President, Founder and CEO, Herbalife International

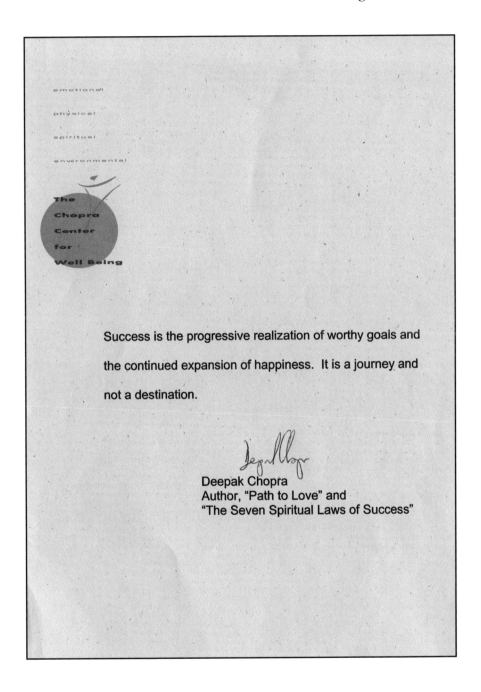

emotional
physical
spiritual
environmental

The Chopra Center for Well Being

Success is the progressive realization of worthy goals and the continued expansion of happiness. It is a journey and not a destination.

Deepak Chopra
Author, "Path to Love" and
"The Seven Spiritual Laws of Success"

Deepak Chopra
Author/Speaker

Mrs. Fields

What Success Means to me

• True Wealth & Success comes when you
are Rich with family, true friends
and loving what you do!

• Success means the greatest failure
is to not try

• Success means an ongoing journey &
never Rest on your laurels

• Success means you feel you made
a positive difference in this
world

Debbie Fields
Founder, Mrs. Fields Cookies

Success means that you live a legacy that your children can always be proud of. ✦

Success means that you left your children with a wonderful Reputation to carry on and pass on. ✦

Debbie Fields
Founder, Mrs. Fields Cookies

JOHN GLENN
OHIO

COMMITTEES:
- GOVERNMENTAL AFFAIRS, CHAIRMAN
- ARMED SERVICES
- SELECT COMMITTEE ON INTELLIGENCE
- SPECIAL COMMITTEE ON AGING

United States Senate

WASHINGTON, DC 20510–3501

November 13, 1995

Thank you for your recent letter asking for my thoughts on success.

I have always said that I have been successful mostly because I was at the right place at the right time, with the preparation I needed to take advantage of that opportunity. If I am now considered a success I think it is not because I set out to become successful but rather because I always tried to do my very best at whatever I attempted. I believe that commitment to ideals, respect for others, and serious study are essential for success in any field. The successful people I most admire are great readers, keen observers and good listeners, and they are curious and questioning about everything -- not always trying to make things go their way, but striving to learn as much as they can about the natural world, and to understand how others see things. Most people, I believe, are capable of being successful if they choose worthwhile goals and prepare themselves for the opportunities they will have.

Best regards.

Sincerely,

John Glenn

John Glenn
United States Senator

John Glenn
Astronaut/U.S. Senator from Ohio

If you think you are beaten, you are;
If you think that you dare not, you don't;
If you'd like to win, but you think you can't,
It's almost certain you won't.

If you think you'll lose, you've lost;
For out in the world you'll find
Success begins with a fellow's will —
It's all in the state of mind.

If you think you are outclassed, you are;
You've got to think high to rise;
You've got to be sure of yourself before
You can ever win a prize.

Life's battles don't always go
To the stronger or faster man;
But soon or late the man who wins
Is the man who thinks he can.

Arnold Palmer
Professional Golfer

BRIAN TRACY INTERNATIONAL

I started off in life with few advantages. I never finished high school, I lived in my car and I worked at laboring jobs for years. When I was 23, I was still working as an itinerant farm worker, 12 hours per day, sleeping in the barn and eating with the farmer's family.

I eventually learned the four key ideas that turned my life around. The first, and most important, was that I was completely responsible for myself, and for everything that happened to me.

This insight eliminated all my excuses, my tendency to blame others for my problems and my seeking for solutions outside of myself.

The second key idea I learned was that I couldn't hit a target I couldn't see. If I didn't know where I was going, any road would get me there. At the age of 24, I began setting clear, written goals for each area of my life. I accomplished more in the following year than I had in the previous 24!

The third idea that changed my life was my discovery that I could learn virtually everything I needed to learn to achieve any goal I could set for myself. I found that almost everyone starts at the bottom and becomes successful by doing what *other* successful people do — until they get the same results.

The fourth idea that moved me from rags to riches, from poverty to affluence, was the importance of persistence and determination in all things.

People succeed because they accept complete responsibility, set clear goals, learn continually and never give up.

It's no miracle. The great secret of success is that there are no *secrets* of success. There are only timeless principles that work for everyone, everywhere. And they will work for *you* when you incorporate these ideas into every area of your life.

Good luck!

Brian Tracy

Brian Tracy
Author/Motivational Speaker

REFLECTIONS

Each person who participated in this book by defining success has succeeded within his or her field of endeavor—whether that be the arts, athletics, business, philanthropy, politics or science. These well-known individuals from all over the world were asked to provide a quote, story, poem or personal experience that defined success to them.

As you read through the contributions, you probably noticed their differences. Some are deeply philosophical; others humorous. Some are straightforward; others poetic. It is interesting to note, too, the similarities. In all instances, the contributors pursued their passions and success found them.

It was my intention to provide these definitions of success in their entirety so that you could envision the countless ways success is defined. It is my hope that within these pages, you have been encouraged to reflect on your own definition of success and what it means in your life.

Every individual, no matter your circumstance, can achieve success. The beauty of life is that we are each free to define success in any way we wish. Always remember that success, as life, is not a destination, but a journey.

Here's to celebrating your success!

CELEBRATING YOUR SUCCESS

It is our hope to include everyone in future volumes of *Celebrating Success*. If you have an inspirational story, poem, cartoon, article or a personal experience that you feel is an example of the spirit of celebrating success, we would love to hear from you!

Simply send your contribution on success to:

Light The Fire Within
P.O. Box 7277
Newport Beach, CA 92658-7277

We will be happy to credit you or the author for your submission. On behalf of The Institute for Successful Living, thank you for participating in *Celebrating Success*.

WHO IS GERARD SMITH?

Gerard Smith is the founder and executive director of The Institute for Successful Living. The institute was founded to provide individuals with the concepts and insights which will inspire them to pursue their dream of successful living.

Gerard is committed to "Giving Back the Dream"—programs designed to help others achieve personal and professional fulfillment. He is a featured motivational speaker at conferences and seminars throughout the world. His areas of expertise include leadership, sales and pursuing entrepreneurial dreams.

After graduating from the University of Southern California, Gerard developed and managed the travel program for the Northrop Corporation, where he creatively reduced annual corporate travel expenses by almost half. He has served on the Board of Governors of the Association of Corporate Travel Executives (ACTE) and the Society of Travel Agents in Government (STAG). He has been the recipient of STAG's Professional Development Award and ACTE's Business Professionalism Award.

Gerard is also a successful businessman and a senior partner of a nationally known travel management consulting firm, The T&E Group, which provides travel management expertise and services to companies and organizations throughout the world. He is frequently quoted and interviewed by such periodicals and news organizations as *Fortune,* the *Washington Post, USA Today,* CNN, and the Associated Press.

Gerard is the author of several books including *The Art of Preferred Hotel Rates* and *Mastering Preferred Hotel Rate Negotiations.* He resides in Newport Beach, California.

ALPHABETICAL INDEX OF CONTRIBUTORS